THE JEWEL IN THE MESS

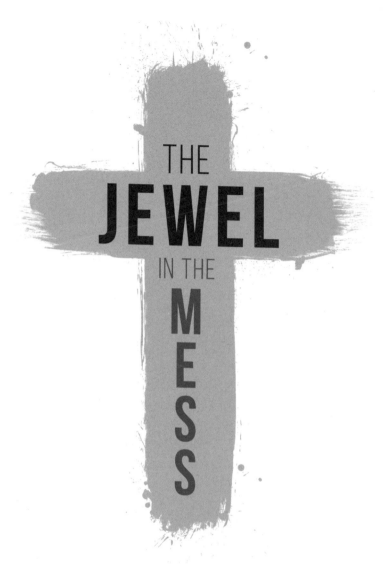

THE JEWEL
IN THE MESS

ALAN ABERNETHY

columba
BOOKS

First published in 2019 by

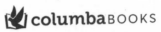 **columba**BOOKS

23 Merrion Square North
Dublin 2, Ireland
www.columbabooks.com

Unless otherwise noted the scripture quotations used throughout are from
the NRSV published by Cambridge University Press, 1992.

Scripture quotations marked (MSG) are taken from *THE MESSAGE.*
Copyright © by Eugene H. Peterson 1993, 2002, 2018. Used by permission
of NavPress. All rights reserved. Represented by Tyndale House
Publishers, Inc.

Quotes from *The Jesus I Never Knew* by Philip Yancey Copyright © 1995
Philip Yancey. Used by permission of Zondervan.

'Stage Fright' from *Watching for the Kingfisher* by Ann Lewin is © Ann
Lewin, 2004, 2006 and 2009. Published by Canterbury Press. Used by
permission. rights@hymnsam.co.uk

ISBN: 978-1-78218-359-4

Set in Linux Libertine 10/14
Cover and book design by Alba Esteban | Columba Books
Printed by Jellysfish Solutions

This book is dedicated with love to those who have loved and
supported me on the journey,
especially my family:

Liz,
Peter, Rosanna and Patrick,
Ruth and Matthew.

CONTENTS

INTRODUCTION

These reflections emerged from over a decade living, praying and working as a bishop; a leader in mission. They have been formed by wrestling with the issues that are facing local parishes, and faithful fellow-disciples, and I have sought to articulate them. In writing I was conscious that I have been influenced by the writings of others, and particularly by the many people I have encountered, who have struggled with church. I offer these reflections prayerfully and in the hope they will help us look to the future with hope and an openness to change.

Having written about Jesus in the mess of our broken humanity I returned from sabbatical last year refreshed and excited to share my own rekindled faith and love for Jesus. Within a month of my return and just after Columba Books had agreed to publish my reflections, I was diagnosed with prostate cancer.

In the course of decades in pastoral ministry, I have journeyed with many people as they have come to terms with a cancer diagnosis and treatment plan. Telling my family and helping others adapt to this news has been a strange and difficult journey, and there is no doubt, as many others have experienced, life changes forever with a cancer diagnosis. Everything is filtered through this new lens and perspectives change. Life will never be the same again. Yet in the midst of the shock and adjustment, we have been very conscious of what I have written about, and that is, that Jesus is present in the mess. We have experienced His presence and peace, not least through the faithful ministry of others, but also in the prayers of so many.

When this book is published, I will be finished chemotherapy and in the middle of radiotherapy treatment. The prognosis is positive and the treatment has already produced excellent results. In the middle of the shock and confusion, I have been given such excellent care and support from my oncologist and all the staff I have met in the

Bridgewater Suite and Cancer Care Unit of the City Hospital, Belfast. They have helped us on this unusual journey and we as a family are very grateful.

This has been such an unexpected and unwelcome journey, but my family and I have found amazing strength from the love we share with each other and the prayers of so many people. I am more convinced than ever, that if our faith makes sense, it must be rooted in the pain, confusion and mess of our lives.

The journey continues and Jesus has promised to be with us. My prayer is that wherever you are, you will discover that Jesus is with you, particularly in your struggles, doubts, questions and mess.

CHAPTER 1

MY JOURNEY

Last year I celebrated a big birthday, one of those birthdays that have a zero attached to the first number. It was indeed my 60th and we had a small family gathering in Donegal, one of our favourite places. There is guaranteed liquid sunshine or soft rain, wild open spaces and so many beaches that there is always one to have to yourself. There was some preparation to have that party, ensuring our son Peter and his wife Rosanna, our daughter Ruth and her husband Matthew could join me and my wife Liz. We booked a house and brought much food with us. The menu was planned and there was even some champagne. It was such a lovely moment and great to celebrate with those I love and cherish. There was lots of walking, eating and laughing.

On reflection, all the major moments of my journey have involved planning and preparation. I remember when I was ordained deacon and priest, many years ago, there was a retreat and many forms to sign and declarations to be made. I also remember the fear and concern as to how I could follow this call. Was I up to it? Would I be able to cope with the expectations and demands of people? How would I be able to help people in pain? There were so many questions that I could not answer and found myself struggling to deal with and yet "it almost seems as if they are a necessary reminder of your need to stay close - very close to Jesus".[1]

The questions were not important, even less the answers, but what mattered was that in some mysterious and amazing way I was seeking to follow Jesus and, by doing so, longing to be with others in the mess of our shared and broken humanity. What mattered to me

---

1   Henri J.M. Nouwen, *The Inner Voice of Love*, (London, D.L.T., 2014), 16.

then was indeed staying close to Jesus. "Jesus is where you are, and you can trust that he will show you the way."[2]

Ordinations were soon followed by marrying Liz who, throughout this journey, has shared so much with me and has helped me understand and live with my own brokenness. Love is a wonderful gift, as it helps us learn to love ourselves and frees us to be who we are meant to be. There was certainly a lot of organisation in a wedding, although having had both our children married within two weeks of each other, I understand even more clearly now the need for planning and preparation.

There was also the moving between two parishes and particularly from a relatively small parish to a growing and busy parish with staff and the need for development. In all of this busyness of ministry there was preparation, although the hardest element of ordained ministry was ensuring that my own spiritual life was kept fresh and deep, that I stayed close to Jesus. The activity of ministry can so often be an excuse for not tending your own inner garden of spiritual fruit and life. It was, and is, a constant tension as the relentless nature of parish life can make it difficult to be what might appear to be selfish and look after yourself or be preparing yourself in order to give. This is not just true for those who are ordained, as there are many in full-time ministry who are not ordained, who also have the struggle of not being recognised and being undervalued, as well as keeping themselves spiritually alive without appropriate support given to them. I would also be concerned about the many faithful people who serve the church in their spare time, and who can be taken for granted as they agree to do more and more jobs. How do they nurture themselves on their faith journey when they are given so much and can receive so little support and nurture?

The next moment in life and ministry was the call to be a bishop, which came suddenly and unexpectedly by a phone call, as this appointment was made by the House of Bishops in the Church of Ireland. Within eight weeks we had left a parish after over 17 years and

2   Ibid., 16.

I was now the person people referred to as "The Bishop". There was preparation for this moment as I went on retreat and had support from fellow-bishops and the people and clergy of Connor diocese. However, nothing could have prepared me for the journey of being bishop.

After three years of seeking to follow this call, I found myself unwell, at first with surgery for gallstones. However, as I prepared to return to work, it became clear that I was emotionally exhausted or burnt out. I had to take further time off and was prescribed anti-depressants. To be diagnosed with a mental health problem was strange, disturbing and confusing. To realise I was suffering from depression was very uncomfortable, as I grew up with the belief that Jesus was all I needed! The spiritual searching, as well as the personal learning, have been stretching. I received so much insight and help on my journey to recovery through cognitive therapy. I discovered that too often I was trying to fix things that were not my fault and taking responsibility for issues, which was unhealthy to do. Much of this struggle stems from my childhood, which was very lonely; there was an unspoken pain that my mum carried and we could not and did not talk about my dad. I am very grateful for the professional help I was given by my doctor and my therapist. As always, my family was amazing and their love a very special gift.

This journey continues and before I was given three months sabbatical to write, pray and recover from the demands of ministry, I had to recognise that I was struggling again with some of the symptoms I experienced before: the anxiety, lack of sleep, tiredness, difficulty in concentrating and the desire to hide and be left alone. I have returned to cognitive therapy and rediscovered that I am constantly in need of recognising the mess within. In this journey of recovery and therapy, I have recognised that throughout my life, I have had a constant sadness that has accompanied me from my childhood with the trauma of my dad leaving my mum, my older brother and me, when I was six years old. There is also the recognition that I have always believed that things must go wrong and that it will be my fault. I have doubted my own ability and always believed that I will be found out as not being good enough. These shadows are now in the light and I am facing them. The important issue for me in this context is that Jesus is present in the very mess of my life to bring grace and healing, which will never end. There is the danger in such a public role and ministry that I could get lost in the role and function to which I have been called. "It is important to tell, at least from time to time, the secret of who we fully are - even if we only tell it to ourselves - because otherwise we run the risk of losing track of who we are truly and fully and little by little come to accept instead the highly edited version which we put forth in hope that the world will find it more acceptable than the real thing."[3]

In writing these reflections on the Jesus that called me to follow, I recognise that that calling has led me to unexpected places, demanding, difficult, painful and exhilarating. The one thing that I have discovered that has been so important is that he has been with me in the mess as much as the wonder. In penning these thoughts, I want to refresh my love and joy in the word made flesh, in the one who is always with us in the mess, even when we find it hard to believe and experience that. In being a bishop, I have certainly seen the church in the brokenness of fallen humanity but also the beauty of being present in the mess. So for me there have been times that I feel my soul has been corroded by the pain of leadership of a church that at times is unwilling to recognise the importance of doing things differently and of recognising that we have so often disconnected from people's everyday lives. "There can be no mission where there is no contact, and many Christians in the West today are imprisoned and isolated by an unnecessary concern for their own sanctification. These bearers of the precious 'treasure' of Christ's presence have become locked into a theological outlook which prevents them from sharing it with the people who are most hungry and 'sick'."[4]

As I rediscover the beauty and love of God made known in Jesus, I want to discover how I can follow Jesus in this amazing and yet

---

3   Frederick Buechner, *Telling Secrets,* (San Francisco, Harper, 1991), 3.
4   Michael Riddell, *Threshold of the Future,* (London, S.P.C.K., 1998), 123.

demanding calling to be a bishop, a leader in mission today. "Sectarian drift has allowed the church to become a private club with high entry requirements; one that is seen as a burden on the backs of ordinary people rather than a sign of hope. In order to be reconciled once again with the world, the church must reorient itself to the sphere where people go about their daily lives."[5]

One of the very important lessons my mum taught me was that she found Jesus in the mess of the chaos she found herself dealing with, through no fault of her own, but because of my dad's gambling addiction. The church found it difficult to deal with the mess as she was now a woman without a husband, a separated lady, a one-parent family. The church in general does find it difficult to deal with people who do not fit into the tidy and expected norm. Yet Jesus was very comfortable with the people on the edge of society and with those who didn't belong. In fact, he was referred to as 'the friend of sinners'. The people he found most difficult were the religious and self-righteous who saw themselves as better than others and found it easy to judge others. There is the constant paradox of the gospel narratives that Jesus is found in the brokenness and pain of people's lives and he finds ways of blessing them without fixing the situation. I believe that Jesus is the jewel in the mess of the world who can help us find blessing and peace in the chaos. However, it is not our task as disciples to fix the mess but somehow by grace and wisdom to live in the mess with others and to find ways of blessing them.

I trust that wherever you are on your journey, you will find Jesus present with you in the mess that it is to be human. "One of the key characteristics of our subsequent life in Christ is the discipline and joy of seeing God as ever-present in the heart of ordinary things. Hopefully we might be seeing the ordinary experiences of life transformed by the presence of a graceful God."[6]

---

5 Ibid., 123.

6 John Pritchard, *Living Jesus*, (London, S.P.C.K., 2017), 91. Reproduced with permission of the Licensor through PLSclear.

CHAPTER 2

THE GIFT

It was a wonderful moment when Liz and I received a WhatsApp from our son Peter and his wife, Rosanna, at 1:15 am on a Tuesday morning in January, to share their news that their son, Patrick Robert was born weighing in at 7lbs 3oz. It was a very emotional time, made all the more real by the photograph that followed of Peter and Patrick. There have been very many photographs since and we have cuddled and held this beautiful new life and special member of two extended families, as the first-born grandchild. I found myself deeply moved by young Patrick. Indeed there were tears of joy and a profound sense of wonder. Becoming and being a grandparent is an incredibly beautiful gift and joy. Liz and I are thoroughly enjoying this new chapter in our lives.

I was struck by the vulnerability of a new-born baby. There was also the wonder of new birth and the joy that this new life has brought. Tiny, helpless and dependent, babies do touch deep emotions within all of us. There is the joy and wonder of being a parent or grandparent. There is the pain of the many couples who cannot have children. We have witnessed too many pictures of children caught up in famine and war not to be touched by the innocence and weakness of children.

The vulnerability and fragility of new life is staggering. These new-born babies are completely dependent upon their parents for everything. In these early stages, they are so dependent upon others for life itself. They cry, feed, have nappies changed and anyone caring for them goes into survival mode. It is such an adjustment and the centre of gravity changes for those given the gift of being parents. There is no escape from this responsibility and there is much advice and counsel, but every baby appears to be different and there is no perfect plan or rule book for being a parent. Above all, parents are to love and nurture this gift to enable them to be able to fly and live life to the full.

The wonder of childbirth is at the heart of the faith I have sought to live out and is at the centre of much of the reflection in this book. I am very grateful for the wonderful gift of Patrick and he has helped me in my reflections on the wonder of that first Christmas, when we believe Jesus came amongst us in the form of a tiny, helpless baby in strange and unusual circumstances. I am concerned that the mystery and awe of this moment are lost in the way we have learnt to celebrate Christmas.

It was always a family day. My mum, my brother and I went to my Auntie Dora and Uncle Ivor's home with my cousins and were joined by my grandparents. My Christmas Day as a child had a regular routine and order of events. Presents were given out before the Queen's speech and the turkey dinner followed. The desserts were always my favourite and there was always a concession for the children who did not want plum pudding, instead they had pavlova or ice cream or indeed both. Television, games, a snooze and even the odd party piece would follow.

Christmas always brings a treasure trove of memories and all the senses are involved: the wonder of Santa Claus, the smell and taste of food, the joy of family and the joy that was tangible among friends, neighbours and strangers. All of this continues in a different format today, but the essence is the same as we love, laugh and give as family and friends. The essence of Christmas is special and it has enabled children to dress up and sing carols and songs for many years. However, one of the dangers is that the school or church nativity play makes it appear to be a fairy story. It certainly misses the strange and bewildering events as they occurred in the life of a family.

My memories of my primary school nativity play are of being dressed in a woollen dressing gown and having a tea towel tied about my head with a school tie. I was one of the shepherds and yet I really wanted to be a wise man. The costumes of the wise men were much more colourful and they were able to bring gifts. I have been to many of these productions and they are always special because of the sheer joy and wonder that children bring to the story.

One that stands out in my memory is when I attended a school in North Belfast as the local bishop. There was a memorable moment when the young boy who was the innkeeper who said "no" to Joseph and Mary decided to go off script and instead of saying that "there was no room in the inn", he used local culture and dialect and told his fellow actors to "Get lost!" He was applauded and after much laughter the story continued without any further additions, as scripted by the staff and practised by the pupils.

Increasingly I find myself irritated by the Christmas cards that paint the perfect scene of the child lying in a manger with the shepherds looking clean and tidy, the wise men beautifully dressed, Mary and Joseph looking radiant and the stable that would pass any rigorous health and safety inspection. "Every Christmas, both Catholics and Protestants send and receive Christmas cards depicting the baby Jesus lying serenely in a perfect carved manger ('no crying he makes'), surrounded by majestically bedecked wise men, crowded under the Byzantine gables of a snow covered stable."[7] In his commentary on the account of the birth of Jesus, Tom Wright observes: "Let's be clear about where they were lodging. Tradition has them knocking at an inn door, being told there was no room, and then being offered the stable along with the animals. But the word for "inn" in the traditional translations has several meanings, and it's likely that they were, in fact, on the ground floor of a house where people normally stayed upstairs. The ground floor would often be used for animals - hence the manger or feeding trough, which came in handy for the baby - but there is nothing to say that there were actually animals there at the time."[8]

As people, we wish each other 'Seasons Greetings' and when we view these images of cleanliness and order something of the original wonder of the incarnation is lost. Jesus was born into the mess of the

7   Michael Frost, *Exiles*, (Michigan, Baker Books, 2006), 35.
8   Tom Wright, *Luke for Everyone*, (London, S.P.C.K., 2001), 21.

world, but the experience must have been so different for those involved in that strange, terrifying and beautiful moment when Christ was born.

As we reflect upon the narrative that we have in the gospel accounts, the events are disturbing and unusual. A young peasant girl is pregnant outside of wedlock and her husband-to-be decides not to disgrace her but to marry her. "Our mental pictures of Mary, aided by centuries of Christian art, place her in late teens or early twenties. Even at that age she would be young - by our standards - for facing the consequences of Gabriel's message to her ... the girl we are talking about was probably no older than 13 and more likely 11 to 12 ... Here is a young girl who, as far as Luke's account records, is asked by God to face disgrace in order to bring salvation to the world."[9]

This young girl is in a strange place and has nowhere to stay after an exhausting journey, not least because she is heavily pregnant. She eventually gives birth and in a place where animals would shelter. This young girl goes through the agonies of childbirth and without any known support gives birth to a son and lays him in a manger or a trough where animals would feed. Although I was present at the birth of both our children, the pain of childbirth is not something I have experienced, but I have witnessed the distress and agony it caused. Mary not only gave birth in a strange place but she did so after all the strange events that occurred leading up to this moment: dreams and angels and a visit to her cousin Elizabeth. As she gave birth in a place where animals would feed, there was no hygienic maternity suite, midwife and someone to deal with a bloody placenta. We have sentimentalised the raw beauty of this moment when we believe God entered the world in all its ugliness and beauty. This is real and tangible incarnation when the word became flesh and dwelt among us. God is in our midst in the mess and confusion of Bethlehem.

The accounts then take further twists and turns as shepherds, who would be considered to be poor and of little standing in the community, were summoned to this scene by angels who sang to them.

9   Paula Gooder, *Journey to the Manger,* (Norwich, Canterbury Press, 2016), 56.

"They were certainly regarded by the rabbis in the Talmud as disreputable and untrustworthy due to their semi-nomadic lifestyle. The problem was that the requirements of caring for flocks meant that they were unable to observe purity laws and often ended up stealing - deliberately or accidentally - by letting their flocks stray on to other people's land. As a result they were regarded as sinners and were ineligible to give evidence in court."[10] These 'sinners' were given a sign to help them discover this wonderful moment and the sign was a 'baby lying in a manger'. This moment is such a critical moment in this eternal love story as God came and lived among us in the chaos and confusion of 1st Century Palestine.

Then there is the account of the wise men from the east, who followed a star and on their way to Bethlehem called with King Herod to discover where the king was born. It is in Matthew's account of the birth of Jesus that we can grasp something of the risk and vulnerability of this birth. "The story of the incarnation is a story of risk inspired by love. So great was God's love for us that he was prepared to risk everything to come to earth as a baby. Not only were there the usual risks of infant mortality but additional risks to Jesus' infant life caused by being who he was. He was born into a world in which people, particularly Herod in this instance, were prepared to do anything to hang onto power they had."[11] As this narrative unfolds, it leads to the slaughter of innocent children in the surrounding countryside because of the jealousy of a powerful person. Even in the middle of this beautiful birth there is the disturbing recognition of the chaos and cruelty of the world. There is the recognition of those who are in power wanting to ensure their survival, whatever the cost. The young family is to experience what it is to be refugees, fleeing for their lives. Jesus is to become the jewel in the mess although his coming does not fix the mess but somehow highlights it and exposes it and also offers hope. The wise men also brought gifts, which would symbolise much of what Jesus would come to represent in his life and ministry.

10   Ibid., 107.
11   Ibid., 127.

This birth is like no other and, like Mary, we are to ponder on these events and learn again and again how they can change our lives as individuals and as faith communities. "The ministry of Mary - being alongside the Christ child, both caring in the midst of vulnerability and standing in awe of divinity, anxious that one is unworthy to be so close to, so trusted with, so touched by the mystery, and yet realising that somehow, in ways beyond one's own desiring, deserving, or comprehending, one has brought forth the fruit of the Spirit and beheld its glory."[12]

It is the ordinariness of this birth that causes us difficulty. "From our perspective, we assume that God's arrival on earth ought to be accompanied by the kind of strange goings-on that we depict in nativity plays: cows that never poop, a baby that never cries, wise men's camels parked in the stable. The one thing we can't bear for Jesus to be is ordinary, for his ordinariness invites us to follow him by providing us with a template of how to be Godlike even as an ordinary human being."[13] I believe we need to rediscover the simplicity, ordinariness and vulnerability of this moment, so we can be in awe at how God has made known his amazing grace in a tiny, helpless and crying baby.

If these events were to unfold today, you could imagine the world's media being present. There would be telephoto lenses and there would be little privacy, as we would want everyone to know how amazing this moment is. Yet this is not the way God planned the birth of Jesus. It happened in a way very few people would know about, although Bethlehem is now famous and much visited by pilgrims. The words of the Christmas Carol sum up the wonder of this moment:

"How silently, How silently,
The wondrous gift is given,
When God imparts to human hearts,
The wonders of His heaven."[14]

---

12 Samuel Wells, *Incarnational Ministry*, (Norwich, Canterbury Press, 2017), 113.

13 Frost, *Exiles*, 37.

14 A verse of the hymn 'O Little Town of Bethlehem' by Phillips Brooks.

There is a choir of angels appearing to the shepherds but nobody will take the words of shepherds seriously as they were from the lower echelons of society. God quietly and unobtrusively came into the world to express the eternal love but somehow that makes it even more difficult for some to believe. However, there is something of the upside down world of God's kingdom taking place in the birth of this baby.

Jane Williams writes: "God's way to draw us back to the real aim of our existence is a strange way. He comes to live with us, as one of us, in utter humility. He is born in fragility and danger, as a human baby, with no wealth or power of privilege to protect him. All the trappings of earth are held at arm's length, so that Jesus can be just what we are, but so often refuse to be - fully human, dependent only upon God the Father."[15]

In today's world of instant and mass communication, the world's media would have been present and Facebook and Twitter would have had millions of hits, but that is not the way God planned it. Jesus came into the world humbly; literally into the mess.

> The God who emerges in the Judaeo-Christian stream is experienced not only in our quiet interior, but in the mess, the wonder and mundanity of everyday living. This was the radical and even shocking idea that was working away in John, eventually welling up in him to produce the stunning opening to his gospel: "And the word became flesh and lived among us, and we have seen his glory, the glory as of a father's son, full of grace and truth." John 1:14 NRSV.[16]

---

15   Jane Williams, *Lectionary Reflections Year A*, (London, S.P.C.K., 2011), 13. Reproduced with permission of the Licensor through PLSclear.
16   Ian Adam, *Cave Refectory Road*, (Norwich, Canterbury Press, 2010), 32-33.

CHAPTER 3

CHILDHOOD

From the confusion and extraordinary events of Bethlehem, this young family is forced to flee to Egypt and become refugees. The fury and rage of a jealous and powerful king led to the deaths of innocent children. This birth that had been unusual is to be overshadowed by the horror of slaughter. From the beginning of this narrative, it is clear that the word became flesh and dwelt among us in the mess and pain of human life and death. There is no quick fix or immediate solution to the struggle and hurt of being human. This incarnation does not bring about instant answers or easy resolution but mysteriously it enters into the awfulness of mess and chaos offering God's amazing grace.

There is no detail given by Matthew in his narrative of how long the family stayed in Egypt, but it is clear from the account that this was an important period of vulnerability and uncertainty for this new family as they began their life together. It is interesting that Matthew makes this connection with Egypt, as this is where the children of Israel escaped from slavery. This baby has come to set people free, as Moses had led the children of Israel out of slavery centuries before. It is fascinating that when the children of Israel came to the edge of the Promised Land and freedom, there were voices asking to go back, as the uncertainty of the new beginning was disconcerting. In our own journey of faith, there is always the danger we want to go back or stand still. This is one of the greatest dangers in the church today, looking backwards to what we imagine to be the best of times, I think this is a form of remembrance which is unhelpful and sees the past through rose-tinted spectacles. Our faith journey must be three dimensional, which remembers the past blessings received, looks to the future with hope and learns to celebrate the present moment. On this journey we are called to keep growing, maturing and changing.

There is also very little detail about the early life of Jesus, except for the family trip to Jerusalem, told by Luke. So the family, on the journey back home, discovered that Jesus was not with them. He was eventually found back in Jerusalem in conversation with the teachers in the temple, causing great consternation to Joseph and Mary.

It is years later in the life of Jesus that the gospel accounts resume the narrative. There are basic facts that we can take from the gospel narratives that are worth noting. "Jesus of Nazareth was a figure of history. He was born somewhere around 4BC and grew up in the town of Nazareth in Northern Palestine. His mother was related to priestly families, and Jesus had a cousin, John, who in the ordinary course of events would have worked as a priest...His later life indicates that, like many Jewish boys, he was from an early age taught to read Israel's ancient scriptures, and by adulthood knew them inside out and had drawn his own conclusions as to what they meant. The strong probability is that he worked with Joseph in the family business, which was the building trade."[17] We will join them in due course, but there is a pause on this journey with Jesus that allows time for personal reflection and reflection on how we have been shaped by our families and community.

I have become increasingly aware of the importance of childhood and the formative years. My own understanding of faith was profoundly shaped by those who nurtured and loved me. My family history meant that my mum's father, my 'poppy', was such an influence of grace and love. He lived his faith with quietness, gentleness and wisdom. Words were only used when necessary, but his influence and demeanour revealed to me the Jesus that I have come to love and follow. My wider family was as supportive and encouraging. My mum's faith was lived out in the context of the pain my father caused, as he was an addictive gambler and we lost everything including our home. He left us when I was six and I was never to see him again. My mum

17   Tom Wright, *Simply Jesus*, (San Francisco, HarperOne, 2011), 8.

had a deep faith and she would often say it was God's providence and the love of family that helped her with no home and two young children. I learnt then that faith does not fix the pain; somehow God was present with us in it. The incarnation was indelibly forged into my faith journey from a very young age. There is always mess in being human and Jesus does not fix the mess but gives grace and blessing in the confusion and struggle. There were times when my mother found the church a difficult place as a woman with no husband and the church found it difficult to deal with the untidiness of her situation. It was easier to keep her at a distance and there were even those who would have doubted her faith and found it easier to walk by on the other side.

Over the years, I have had to spend much time reflecting upon my childhood and how it has shaped me in so many ways. There has been a shadow of sadness that has hung over me from childhood, unresolved grief for what I lost. I was blessed with so much, but yet the fundamental relationship with my mum was fractured by my dad's illness and his inability to deal with it. She was a special lady and would do without to give us anything we needed. Her care for us was amazing, but she could not offer emotional support because of her own pain and hurt. The damage to trust was deep and lasting. It made her cautious and fearful which she passed on to me. I have carried unhelpful anxiety throughout my journey because the expectation was deep within that things will go wrong. She also protected me from thinking that I was special. The expectation for me was never very high. As I have journeyed with depression and cognitive therapy, I have had to recognise that I have a core belief that I am not good enough. There has also been the shadow of believing that if something goes wrong then it is my fault and I have to fix it. When I was growing up, there was never the recognition that children were profoundly affected by marriage break up and the pain of what essentially was a bereavement. I still would be concerned today as to how the struggle of children in the context of relationship breakdown can be ignored or used by either or both parents. It is years later that I have learnt to grieve for what I didn't have. In all of this, I have found it very important to be very conscious of Jesus, present with me in the mess and pain of my life, bringing blessing and peace. The grace and mercy do not fix the pain and sort out my past, but they bring blessing, learning and growth that in turn can bring blessing to others. For my dear mum, death came to her as a friend after a few weeks in hospital. I found it a moment of healing for her, although I have been on a journey of discovery since. She had watched her two boys make a life for themselves and become parents, her work was done and she had made the best of very difficult circumstances. I find the words of Ed Sheeran's song helpful and healing:

> "Hallelujah, You were an angel
> in the shape of my mum
> you got to see the person that
> I have become
> Spread your wings and I know
> That when God took you back,
> he said Hallelujah
> you're home"[18]

As I reflect upon Mary, the mother of Jesus, I am in awe of her and wonder at her gentle, gracious and humble spirit that became a channel for God's amazing grace in the gift of the word made flesh.

> "He began so small,
> curled in the pulsing dark
> of the womb of a girl
> frightened one morning by an angel,
> finding herself prematurely breathing heaven.
> He was safe there,
> guarded against the girl's poverty,
> with just enough for his growing,

---

18   Ed Sheeran, 'Supermarket Flowers'.

oblivious to her threatening disgrace,
warmed by her defiance."[19]

This amazing miracle of grace was brought to us through this ordinary and yet extraordinary young girl who, in the midst of bewilderment, disgrace and fear, became a channel for the wonder of incarnation. God became present in the mess and brought such blessing and grace into the world through the obedience and love of Mary. Within my own tradition of church, this very special young girl has been undervalued. Throughout the gospel narratives she is there watching, observing and loving. She is there at the end watching him die and surely there is no greater pain than a parent watching a child die. This remarkable woman is critical to this moment when God came among us to declare his unending love for humanity and the created order. It is one of the great paradoxes of the scriptures that God takes the ordinary and makes it special.

These years of family life and the learning of faith at the centre of family and community are assumed when it comes to our understanding of the life of Jesus. These are critical years of preparation and yet they are the silent years as far as the gospel narratives are concerned.

As I reflect on my own journey of faith, I am conscious of the many people who helped me grasp faith and see it in action. I have to recognise that there were also influences that made me see some of the negative aspects of faith as I witnessed them in church and in community. Growing up in Belfast during the Troubles was formative, as I witnessed the raw sectarianism of religion and also the quiet enduring faith of grace and relationship. These tensions still run deep in the psyche of community life in Northern Ireland. Over the years, there are many faithful pilgrims who have modelled grace and friendship across religious and political divides, although there is still a deep fear of the 'other' that can trip us up in our search for peace and reconciliation. It can be all too easy to demonise the 'other'.

19   Trevor Dennis, *God Treads Softly Here*, (London, S.P.C.K, 2004), 7. Reproduced with permission of the Licensor through PLSclear.

In my years in ordained ministry and perhaps more especially as bishop, I have been able to observe how some people have sought to change the culture and challenge the community to a better way. "The best culture changers bear no banners; they sound no trumpets. Their ends are sweeping but their means are mundane. They are firm in their commitments, yet flexible in the ways they fulfil them. Their actions may be small but can spread like a virus. They yearn for rapid change but trust in patience. They often work individually but pull people together. Instead of stridently pressing their agenda, they start conversations. Rather than battling powerful foes, they seek powerful friends. And in the face of setbacks they keep going."[20]

I am very grateful for the many people who have helped shape me in my faith journey and showed me the loveliness of Jesus. In the confusion and mess of growing up in a society riddled with pain and tension, there are many victims. I am conscious as to how the faith can be used to justify thinking and action that I find difficult to square with the Jesus I have come to know and love. However, I am also very grateful for the many ordinary people who have done extraordinary things equipped and enriched by the grace of Jesus. He has blessed them and so many others through them in the mess of our broken and hurting society.

The greatest difficulty in a religious society is the inability to see our own brokenness as we are too busy seeing everybody else's fault. "For as long as we insist on maintaining safe moral grids in which we always know where we stand (and where everyone else stands!), these poses of self sufficiency, we disenfranchise ourselves from the company of the found sheep, the found coin, the two found brothers, and the celebration angels."[21]

In penning these reflections, I am very conscious of my own need for this amazing grace and indeed in revisiting this incredible life of Jesus, it is good to be reminded of his humanity and that he was

20   Debra Myeson, 'Harvard Business Review' quoted in Neil Hudson, *Imagine Church,* (Illinois, InterVarsity Press, 2012).
21   Eugene Peterson, *Tell it Slant,* (Michigan, Eerdmans, 2008), 98.

indeed, the word made flesh. He walks with us in all our brokenness and yet is the constant reminder that we are made in the image of God. He reveals to us the full potential of our humanity as we recognise our brokenness and accept his amazing gift of grace.

CHAPTER 4

THE BEST MAN

Throughout this book, my reflections are based upon the four gospels as the main sources to understanding and meditating upon the life of Jesus. My own faith journey in prayer, study and conversation, with trusted friends, has helped shaped my thinking. These have been enriched by visiting places and people who are seeking to incarnate the presence of Jesus today in some difficult and complex human situations with people who are all made in the image of God. At the present moment, my words are also profoundly influenced by my ministry as someone called to be a leader in mission in the church today.

One of the frustrations that I experienced as an ordinand, was the disconnect between study and practice. There were many important questions surrounding the gospels and how they were written and yet these questions did not help me in being with people in the pain and hurt of their experiences. This is not the place for a detailed study of the sources of the gospels and the historicity of the accounts we have in the gospels.

There has to be the recognition that all accounts that we have offer interpretation. "Our earliest and best sources for knowing about Jesus are already interpretations; there is no way they could not be."[22] Each of the four gospels gives us a different view of what I believe to be the jewel that is Jesus. They reflect different ways of expressing the miracle that was the incarnation, as Jesus lived a fully human life. The Jesus I have come to know, love and follow was this person and the mystery is that he was the word made flesh. The incarnation is a mystery and though it is difficult to comprehend, it is even more difficult for many to believe. I want to journey again with him in reflecting

---

22 Peterson, *Tell it Slant*, 6.

upon his life and renew my own faith and to be challenged afresh as to how I can bless people in the mess of what it is to be human.

The immediacy and urgency of Mark's account have a speed and directness. The pace of narrative is grasped when you can read it all at once. There is no birth narrative but we begin with the preaching of John the Baptist. "Many people think Mark's gospel was the first to be written, and certainly it has all the zip and punch of a quick, hasty story that's meant to grab you by the collar and make you face the truth about Jesus, about God, and about yourself."[23] This is the good news as told by Mark and from the beginning he declares his agenda.

It is Luke and Matthew who give us the birth narratives and yet they have their own particular interpretation of the life of Jesus as they record it. "Luke tells us that he had had a chance to stand back from the extraordinary events that had been going on, to talk to people involved, to read some earlier writings, and to make his own full version so that readers could know the truth about the things to do with Jesus."[24] One of my favourite stories in the gospels is recorded by Luke and that is the story of the prodigal son. "Matthew's gospel presents Jesus in a rich, many-sided way. He appears as the Messiah of Israel, the king who will rule and save the world. He comes to us as a teacher greater than Moses."[25] The incredible words of the Beatitudes are recorded by Matthew and the teaching that follows has inspired and challenged millions of followers of Jesus for centuries. I will be reflecting on the teaching of Jesus in a later chapter and I have found myself continually wanting to learn from his storytelling that leaves us to work out what he is saying rather than spoon-feeding his listeners.

It is the opening words of John's gospel that have always inspired me and left me in awe at what happened in Bethlehem those centu-

---

23 Tom Wright, *Mark for Everyone*, (London, S.P.C.K., 2001), x. Reproduced with permission of the Licensor through PLSclear.

24 Wright, *Luke for Everyone*, x. Reproduced with permission of the Licensor through PLSclear.

25 Tom Wright, *Matthew for Everyone*, (London, S.P.C.K., 2001), x. Reproduced with permission of the Licensor through PLSclear.

ries ago. These are words that I have read at midnight Eucharists in parish churches and cathedrals so many times. They always make me ponder at the mystery of the incarnation. "In the beginning was the word, and the word was with God, and the word was God."[26] This prologue to the gospel is placing Jesus clearly and unmistakably as part of the eternal story of God's amazing love for the created order. We are transported back to the beginning of Genesis and the beginning of creation. This is 'the story' of God's desire and hope for all that has been created. As Jesus became human in the word made flesh, we can now see what God is like by looking at Jesus. "The word became flesh and blood, and moved into our neighbourhood." (MSG)

Jesus came into the confusion and pain of what it is to be human and blessed many as he journeyed in 1st Century Palestine. John's gospel "gives the appearance of being written by someone who was a very close friend of Jesus, and who spent the rest of his life mulling over, more and more deeply, what Jesus had done and said and achieved, praying it through from every angle, and helping others understand it."[27]

It is John the Baptist who sets the scene for the ministry of Jesus and he is the beginning of the good news as presented by Mark. Those listening to John were not expecting a call to repentance. They had wanted a Messiah, someone who would free them from Roman rule. They were expecting another deliverance from foreign rule as they had in the Exodus when they were delivered from Egypt and eventually made it to the Promised Land. However, they were being asked to repent in preparation for someone who was coming and John's role was to make people ready for his coming.

John was very clear what his calling was: he was not the Messiah, but was preparing the way for him. Vocation comes from the Latin *vocare*, and it is the work we are called to by God. This is a subject with which many disciples wrestle. I have sought to follow a vocation

---

26   John 1:1 NRSV.
27   Tom Wright, *John for Everyone*, (London, S.P.C.K., 2002), x. Reproduced with permission of the Licensor through PLSclear.

to ordained ministry. There are times when I have struggled with this calling because of how frustrating the church can be. Like any large institution, it has a built-in capacity to struggle with change and to accept the status quo. My experience in parish life as a rector taught me that people complain about change and this was made more complicated particularly by some religious people who spent a great deal of their time judging others as not belonging or not coming up to the mark.

As a bishop it has been even more frustrating, as there is the assumption that a bishop has power, but essentially, by the constitution of the Church of Ireland, a bishop has authority but not power. We are a church governed by General Synod and committees. All the available facts and figures show that we are in decline yet, in my experience, there is much denial about the reality and there is the assumption that everything will be fine. In many places, the local church has little engagement with people in the local community and the parish church is often seen as a strange and unwelcoming place. Increasing numbers of people view the church as irrelevant and not connecting with their daily lives. My vocation has certainly been tested in the last number of years. I have found myself weary in spirit as I seek to lead and give direction to the enormous challenge that is ours. However, I believe that God wants us to find ways of being missional and connecting with the ordinariness and mess of people's lives. Yet so much of our energy and time is spent maintaining the machinery of church. Within my role of oversight, I increasingly see the need for the church, particularly in a local community, to be in the mess of people's lives seeking to find ways of bringing God's blessing. Somehow as we do this, we will find the opportunity to share the amazing grace that we have experienced in Jesus.

One of the tensions of vocation in my religious upbringing was the tension between enjoying God's will for our lives and the suggestion that we could only be following God's will if it was difficult and costly. The emphasis that I heard was that this calling was always very costly and I did not hear much about joy. This is something I now find deeply unhelpful. John the Baptist had a difficult calling, but he appears to be more than content to be the one directing people to Jesus. I want to affirm that the call of God will lead us to challenge but also joy! "The place God calls you to is the place where your deep gladness and the world's deep hunger meet."[28]

The message of repentance was one of challenge and is still one that needs to be heard today. However, it is difficult to be able to proclaim this without sounding harsh and judgemental. The message as proclaimed by John the Baptist was for the people who came to hear him. The people of his day were called to stop rebelling against the living God. In each and every generation repentance is an essential part of a journey with God as we discover his grace in Jesus. "Repentance is a difficult word to hear. Repentance is a complex thing. It simply means 'turn around' or 'change your mind', the word is without ambiguity. Just do it. Personally but not individualistically. In the biblical story repentance cannot be narrowed down to something private, such as being sorry for your sins and ready to make amends. The call is to return to God and the ways of his people. To return to the Story and everything and everyone in the Story. It has to do with entering a new way of life, taking up membership in the kingdom of God."[29]

John the Baptist has such a critical part in the narrative, but his role is also very clear: he is to point people to Jesus. "Wherever John the Baptist appears in this gospel, he directs people to Jesus. It is made clear he is 'not the light' himself, but a 'witness to the light'. He does not even mind when his followers complain that Jesus is baptising more people, saying 'He must increase and I must decrease'."[30] What a delightful calling it is to point people to Jesus. This is the calling of individual disciples and essentially it is the calling of every local Christian faith community. This is a very urgent message for those of us who seek to be disciples today within the life of the local

28   Frederick Buechner, *Listening to your Life*, (San Francisco, HarperOne, 1992), 186.
29   Peterson, *Tell it Slant*, 118-9.
30   Richard A. Burridge, *John: The People's Bible Commentary*, Lambeth Conference Edition, (Oxford, B.R.F., 2008), 20.

church. We must find ways of engaging with people among whom we are called to live and discover ways of pointing them to Jesus. This is best done by incarnating his presence, which will mean taking our eyes off maintaining our local church and looking to serve people in the mess of what it is to be human. Too often we want to bring people to join us in our gatherings in local churches when our calling is to be among them in the chaos and untidiness of each and every local community. We are not there to fix them or to make them like us but, rather, to help them discover the loveliness of Jesus and this, in today's culture, is best done initially without words but by service.

CHAPTER 5

STRUGGLE

The gospel narratives are a wonderful resource for reflection and learning. Each account helps us see a different aspect of this jewel that is
Jesus. We have just been reflecting on the ministry of John the Baptist
and the rest of the narratives focus on the ministry of Jesus that leads to
his crucifixion and ultimately to the new beginning of resurrection. In
the synoptic tradition, the baptism of Jesus happens before the temptations. The baptism of Jesus is that holy moment of affirmation from the
Father, as Jesus begins his public ministry and accepts his calling to do
the Father's will. It is a fascinating moment, which is followed by being
in the real human struggle of temptation. There is no escape for Jesus
from what is his calling to be in the mess of humanity and helping us
see what God is like in human form. "Jesus is our primary revelation
that God is personal, extravagantly personal. When we deal with God,
we are not dealing with a spiritual principle, a religious idea, an ethical
issue, or a mystical feeling. We are dealing personally with Jesus, who
is dealing personally with us."[31]

The temptations are the moment when we glimpse the shadow of
the struggle and the reality of what lies ahead. The ministry of Jesus
is not just that of a great teacher or a good man, but he is involved in
the ultimate battle between good and evil. The narratives record the
temptations differently. Mark, with his usual brevity, states that Jesus
was "in the wilderness forty days, tempted by Satan; and he was with
the wild beasts; and the angels waited on him".[32] Matthew and Luke
give us slightly more detail and mention three specific temptations,
but place them in a different order. Following Mark's example of

31 Peterson, *Tell it Slant*, 44.
32 Mark 1:12 NRSV.

brevity, they were essentially about food, love and power. I believe that the temptation about power is still one of the most relevant in today's culture and indeed even within the life and witness of the church. Temptation is something everyone can understand, but it is difficult to get the right balance in living with this inner battle. Guilt is so destructive and when we fail, as we will, it is easy to wallow in our broken humanity. My own experience in growing up in a context of church and Sunday School was to be told, very often, that I was a miserable sinner and I constantly needed to repent, this can easily become self-loathing. I do need to repent constantly, but I am also made in the image of God and have that potential within me that God is seeking to restore by his grace. "The Christian discipline of fighting temptation is not about self-hatred, or rejecting parts of our God-given humanity. It is about celebrating God's gift of full humanity and, like someone learning a musical instrument, discovering how to tune it and play it to its best possibility."[33]

This tension is not just true as we remember the temptations of Jesus but it is vital in the way we seek to engage with people. If we can remember that everyone is made in the image of God, we are less likely to become judgemental and self-righteous. We will also be able to come alongside people without believing that our primary task is to fix them or make them more like us. Jesus wants to be with all of us in our brokenness and help us discover his grace and give us the freedom of becoming fully human, as made in the image of God. For each of us, this will be different, as every person is unique and special.

For me, an integral part of my journey with Jesus has been discovering what makes me who I am and learning that I have the opportunity not to stay rooted in the past but to learn how the future can be different by his grace. All of us have our own story in terms of our genes, our childhood and the culture that shaped us. My own story has meant that I have learnt some painful lessons as an adult that began in my childhood. These lessons never end as I seek to be free of the thought patterns and behaviour that I learnt as a child. I

---

33   Wright, *Luke for Everyone*, 44.

have always found it hard to enjoy the present because I am anxious about what might go wrong and my core belief from childhood is that things always go wrong. This shadow has haunted me and at times controlled me. It is also accompanied by a lack of self-confidence in my own worth and value. The most important lesson has been to discover that Jesus has been with me on this journey and he believes in me and wants to help me experience the joy of the present moment. "Self-knowledge, which can hurt like hell at times, is nevertheless essentially joyful. And always has the element of surprise."[34]

There have been some helpful tips that have aided me on this journey. I have had to learn to be more compassionate with myself and be able to keep a scrapbook of letters I have received when people have thanked me for bringing them God's blessing. It has also been very helpful to find at least three things every day for which I am thankful, my own daily, personal psalm of praise. These records help me find ways of seeing myself as someone who even through my broken humanity can be used by God to bring his extraordinary blessing. It is a biblical pattern that God takes the ordinary and makes it special. This is true of water, bread, wine, the wood of a cross, a tomb given by a stranger, and the many people throughout the story of God's loving purposes, who, despite their ordinariness, were made special by God. "You can trust yourself because God trusts you, using your journey, your experience. Nothing will be wasted; all has been forgiven; nothing will be held against you."[35]

My experience of being a disciple is one of constantly recognising that I have so much still to learn and that the greatest gift I bring is my vulnerability and brokenness; "we do not really know God except through our broken and rejoicing humanity."[36] I find encouragement when I see the disciples who were called to

34 Laurence Freeman, *Jesus: The Teacher Within*, (Norwich, Canterbury Press, 2010), 65.

35 Richard Rohr, *Everything Belongs*, (New York, The Crossroad Publishing Company, 1999), 129.

36 Ibid., 19.

follow Jesus; they were an eclectic bunch and it is their ordinariness that is inspiring. "Jesus does not seem to choose his followers on the basis of native talent or perfectibility or potential for greatness. When he lived on earth he surrounded himself with ordinary people who misunderstood him, failed to exercise much spiritual power, and sometimes behave like churlish children."[37] It is important to note their amazing willingness to follow, to give up everything for someone whom they had just met. He inspired them and drew them to a very different life and their lives would never be the same again. It is this Jesus that I am seeking to follow. There are many who have found the church a difficult place and the church has not always behaved in appropriate ways, as it is full of broken people. We need to confess our self-righteousness, our pomposity and arrogance and recognise that sometimes this is what people have encountered. However, I want to point anyone who has struggled with church, or who has been hurt by the church and finds it hard to believe, to look at the jewel in the mess and see Jesus.

It is this Jesus who inspired me when I set out many years ago on a journey to ordination. I struggled with that call and had it not been for others encouraging and nagging me, I am sure I would have found excuses to run away from this particular calling. This calling has led me to some fascinating, demanding and painful places, but deep within; it is based on this jewel who is Jesus. However, it is important for me to be reminded that my first call is to be a disciple, a learner. "The disciples were called to a life-time of learning and while they were learning, before they had even understood some of the vital things they needed to grasp (like who Jesus was and what he had come to do), Jesus sent them out in the service of the kingdom."[38]

I am also very grateful for those friends who have helped disciple me. One of the strange ironies that I discovered when I was ordained is that there appeared to be the assumption that I was now an expert

37   Philip Yancey, *The Jesus I Never Knew*, (Michigan, Zondervan, 1995), 100.
38   Paula Gooder, *Everyday God*, (Norwich, Canterbury Press, 2012), 108.

on matters of faith and it might have been easy to forget that I was still a disciple, someone who was always learning. This was all the more apparent when I was ordained a bishop. It can be a lonely place, as you are the one who is the overseer and carry the double-edge role of being pastorally responsible, but also the one who has to exercise discipline. I constantly have to remind myself that my primary calling is to be a disciple of Jesus. It is critical that all of us who seek to follow Jesus, no matter where we exercise our discipleship and ministry, find ways of being disciples and of discipling others.

One of the greatest weaknesses of the established churches in the last century is that we have failed to make disciples. We have been very good at baptising, marrying, burying and offering pastoral care, but we have been too dependent upon the professional ordained and non-ordained ministries and have not helped and equipped every follower of Jesus in their daily discipleship. Therefore, we have sought innovative and creative ways of getting people to church when actually our responsibility is to get the people who worship every week equipped to be Jesus in their workplace, communities and homes. This is not to say that many faithful people have not sought to do this, but our emphasis has been wrong. We have been busy keeping our local parish structures going and our energy has been on buildings, finance, committees and we have neglected the essential calling of the church, which is to make disciples and to be intentional in doing so.

In my own ministry, I also have to confess I have not placed enough emphasis upon my own personal discipleship. I have sought to nurture my prayer life and rule of life, but I believe discipleship is also about accountability to fellow-disciples and to ensure I am still growing in faith and continuing to develop the God-given gifts I have been given. This is something I do want to find ways of changing, but I am also concerned about how within the institutional churches we find ways of making disciples. This is critical because if we are going to connect with those who do not or will not come to church, we need everyone who lives and works in these communities to be equipped and supported to bring the blessing and presence of Jesus to all. In my observations, I see many local churches disconnected from their local communities, although I am encouraged by the number of parishes that are seeking to find ways of serving and connecting with local areas and groups. "Traditionally when we have been together, we have spent most of our time encouraging one another to concentrate on the gathered activities of church life. This is obviously significant, but has meant that we have limited our understanding of church to a particular place, time and set of activities."[39] The danger is that we spend all our time and energy on the local church and the programme and lose sight of the fact that we are here for those who do not belong, and may even feel excluded. It also creates an unhealthy disconnect between our church life and our everyday life and makes it more difficult to connect with people in the mess of everyday life and community.

It is encouraging to remember that Jesus entrusted the mission of God to a motley bunch who had been called to be disciples by him and they turned the world upside down as they set out to declare the amazing grace and love of God made known in Jesus. These disciples had been given such an example, in being with Jesus, watching and learning, and their energy and passion flowed from their deep relationship of love with Jesus. They were not caught up in church structures or maintaining buildings but had a freedom to live out their message in local communities and by building relationships. I envy them this freedom and somehow today we need to rediscover the importance of relationship that flows from the one who has called us.

I have always been very fond of Peter; he often says what others are probably thinking and he wears his heart on his sleeve. His background as a fisherman gave him determination and the ability to keep going. I find the following reflection on this disciple very helpful in my own journey with Jesus: "I think Jesus chose fishermen for a good reason. To be part of his uprising, we must be willing to fail a lot, and

---

39   Neil Hudson, *Imagine Church*, (Illinois, InterVarsity Press, 2012), 44-5.

to keep trying. We will face long, dark nights when nothing happens. But we can never give up hope. He caught us in his net of love, so we go and spread the net for others. And so, fellow disciples, let's get moving. Let us walk the road with Jesus."[40]

---

40   Brian McLaren, *We make the Road by Walking*, (London, Hodder and Stoughton, 2014), 220.

being good enough. These shadows are now in the light and I am facing them. The important issue for me in this context is that Jesus is present in the very mess of my life to bring grace and healing, which will never end. There is the danger in such a public role and ministry that I could get lost in the role and function to which I have been called. "It is important to tell, at least from time to time, the secret of who we fully are – even if we only tell it to ourselves – because otherwise we run the risk of losing track of who we are truly and fully and little by little come to accept instead the highly edited version which we put forth in hope that the world will find it more acceptable than the real thing."[3]

In writing these reflections on the Jesus that called me to follow, I recognise that that calling has led me to unexpected places, demanding, difficult, painful and exhilarating. The one thing that I have discovered that has been so important is that he has been with me in the mess as much as the wonder. In penning these thoughts, I want to refresh my love and joy in the word made flesh, in the one who is always with us in the mess, even when we find it hard to believe and experience that. In being a bishop, I have certainly seen the church in the brokenness of fallen humanity but also the beauty of being present in the mess. So for me there have been times that I feel my soul has been corroded by the pain of leadership of a church that at times is unwilling to recognise the importance of doing things differently and of recognising that we have so often disconnected from people's everyday lives. "There can be no mission where there is no contact, and many Christians in the West today are imprisoned and isolated by an unnecessary concern for their own sanctification. These bearers of the precious 'treasure' of Christ's presence have become locked into a theological outlook which prevents them from sharing it with the people who are most hungry and 'sick'."[4]

As I rediscover the beauty and love of God made known in Jesus, I want to discover how I can follow Jesus in this amazing and yet

3   Frederick Buechner, *Telling Secrets*, (San Francisco, Harper, 1991), 3.
4   Michael Riddell, *Threshold of the Future*, (London, S.P.C.K., 1998), 125.

CHAPTER 6

STORY TELLER

I remember it vividly and ever since I have loved reading. *The Otterbury Incident*, by Cecil Day Lewis, was a novel that gripped me with the delight and joy of storytelling. As a child of eight, I was caught up in the story and had vivid images of the various characters. This is a fascinating story, set in the imaginary village of Otterbury, just after the Second World War. There are rival gangs, campaigns to raise money, a diligent headmaster and delightful sub plots and gentle morality. It is the first book that really gave me a lifelong love of stories and novels.

Growing up in Northern Ireland also taught me the craic and escapism that comes from storytelling. Despite the fact of our turbulent and violent history, anyone from Ireland, north or south, has the great capacity to laugh at themselves. It has been part of our ability to cope with the conflict and pain many have experienced. There is a certain Belfast irony and humour that we have one of the most famous tourist attractions in Europe, remembering the Titanic, a wonderful cruise liner, built in Belfast, which tragically sank.

When I first found myself intrigued by Jesus, it was the stories, the parables, that fascinated me. They were not religious in content and left room for imagination and probing. They dealt with everyday and ordinary things. Many of the sermons I heard as a child and young person were arid and lacked the energy and creativity of the stories Jesus told. "Everyone likes a good story, and Jesus' knack for storytelling held the interest of a mostly illiterate society of farmers and fishermen. Since stories are easier to remember than concepts or outlines, the parables also helped preserve his message: years later when people reflected on what Jesus had taught, his parables came to mind in vivid detail."[41] Our daughter-in-law Rosanna's parents own a working farm and recently when we were visiting Robert and Sue, I was intrigued to see the wheat crop as there were weeds riddled through this healthy crop - an everyday symbol of the wheat and the tares growing together. It is this storytelling rooted in the everyday that draws us to the ordinariness of the parables. Yet they are everyday stories that lead us to discover so much more as we wrestle with them.

The parables are usually without any obvious religious importance. These are stories for people who would not have listened to God-talk but who were intrigued by how Jesus, the storyteller, told stories that connected with their everyday lives and allowed them space to probe and question. There must be lessons here for those who have to talk about Jesus today in a culture that does not want to hear pious jargon and is tired of religious clichés.

It is impossible to describe this amazing, eternal love of God made known in a baby born in Bethlehem. However, the image of a shepherd leaving 99 sheep to find the one that is lost speaks of a madness in leaving his sheep vulnerable to attacks from wild animals or thieves. The image of a distraught father who is waiting for a son to return, causes the older brother rightly to question the unfairness of such love. Stories or parables leave room for the imagination and probing that concepts can never give us. "It is one thing to talk in abstract terms about the infinite, boundless love of God. It is quite another to tell of a man who lays down his life for his friends, or of a lovesick father who scans the horizon every night for some sign of a wayward son."[42]

This parable is one that has become such an important part of my journey with Jesus and my faith story. I can identify with the prodigal who needs to recognise the need for going home and finding a welcome and love unrestrained there. As someone who lost my father at such a young age, I have also struggled with the concept of a 'loving father'.

41   Yancey, *The Jesus I Never Knew*, 95.
42   Yancey, *The Jesus I Never Knew*, 95.

This parable has helped me grasp the amazing grace and love portrayed by the father in this story, who never stops loving the wayward son. There is also a very helpful reminder in this delightful story of how this amazing grace made known to us in Jesus is unjust. The older brother is a reminder to any disciple of Jesus that God's love knows no bounds and may appear as unfair, especially to those who serve others and give so freely and willingly. It is always difficult for any group of Christians not to become self-righteous and want to be careful as to who is allowed to join or become part of the faith community. One of the most important tensions being discovered in the new expressions of church is that people want to belong before they believe. Community is something that is desperately needed in what can be a very lonely and impersonal culture today. I have experienced a church that wants people to believe before they belong. This is a real and important question that we need to wrestle with as we as faith communities seek to be missional. God's love will always disturb us and push us to places that will be uncomfortable as this amazing love is offered to all.

One of the joys of reading is that I can build a mental image or picture of the characters and the scenes that are described. I always try to read a novel before I watch it portrayed in a movie or serialised in television drama. When reading, I want to let my imagination paint its own pictures. One of the joys of the stories that Jesus told is that he invites the hearers to enter the world he is creating by his storytelling. The hearer is valued by Jesus; he wants the hearer to enter the story and to wrestle with it and to allow space and time for the hearer to find themselves caught up in the story. "Inconspicuously, even surreptitiously, a parable involves the hearer. This brief, commonplace, unpretentious story is thrown into a conversation and lands at our feet, compelling notice. A parable is not ordinarily used to tell us something new but to get us to notice something that we have overlooked although it has been right there before us for years."[43]

In the context that Jesus told the stories, there was always a connection with his calling. The parables were challenging the religious

---

43   Peterson, *Tell it Slant*, 19.

order of the day and announcing the kingdom. "They were stories designed to tease, to clothe the shocking and revolutionary message of God's kingdom in garb that left the hearers wondering, trying to think it out, never quite able (until near the end) to pin Jesus down. They were stories full of echoes. They resonated with ancient scriptural promises; they reminded their hearers of Israel's future hopes and claimed by implication that these hopes were now being realised, even if in the way they had not imagined."[44] Many of the stories leave the hearer to imagine an ending. The parables leave us to wrestle and discover what is this story telling us about God and the kingdom of God. The stories were announcing something different about God's revelation to the world made known in Jesus. As he tells the stories, the hearer is left to discover the challenge of what is being said. I find this refreshing from my early years of faith when I was told what to believe and how to behave, instead of being discipled and equipped to discover with fellow-disciples what these stories are saying to us today.

The stories also lead us to another place where we can wrestle with what they mean and are saying to us today. "His parables did more than reflect or describe the world in which he lived; rather, they enabled Jesus to create worlds. This is because parables are open, deliberately not accidentally, to more than one level of interpretation."[45] This wrestling with them is important as we seek to understand the message of God's kingdom that Jesus was declaring. I have been very concerned, through many years in ordained ministry, that there is an expectation that my role as the professional minister is to instruct and to tell people what to believe. One of the dilemmas in traditional church life is how we have taken people out of context and sent them to a theological college or seminary to train them for ministry. However, these people should already have been ministering and we disconnect them from their context and ministry and in essence to professionalise them. A danger in doing so is that many people in

44 Wright, *Simply Jesus*, 88.
45 Ed Kessler, *Jesus: Pocket GIANTS*, (Gloucestershire, The History Press, 2016), 41.

parish churches assume these trained ministers are the experts and have all the answers to faith and discipleship. We are all disciples learning what it is to follow Jesus today in rapidly changing communities and culture. This means that much of our preaching and teaching has left little room for questioning and probing especially when the preacher is uninterrupted and not able and maybe unwilling to take questions in many contexts of worship. "Sadly so much of what passes for Christian teaching takes all the looking out of the picture. It eliminates searching, closes down our options, answers all our questions, and leaves us needing to know no more (or worse, wanting to know no more). Just about any institution these days recognises that the way to motivate, teach, or mobilise its people is to engage them in an active process of discovery. Just about every institution bar the church, that is. Learning is more effective when it's an active process on the part of the learner instead of a passive one."[46]

I am increasingly of the opinion that we need to revisit how we train those who are offering themselves for ordained ministry and find ways of training them in a particular local context alongside the people and the issues that are of relevance. We need to help people discover that above all else they are fellow-disciples in incarnating the presence of Jesus in each and every local community. This is being done by Church Army in the training of pioneer evangelists and is perhaps a model that will emerge with the new model of ordained local ministry in the Church of Ireland.

The tenor of Jesus in his storytelling is something that has always enthralled me. Anyone listening is respected and valued and given the space to take the story and let it connect with them, wherever they are on their own spiritual journey. There is a challenge in every parable and sometimes the challenge is stark. I always find the parable of the sheep and the goats leaves me feeling very uncomfortable. I also find it strange that sheep get the best deal, as I personally prefer goats. However, Jesus in his culture knew the importance and value of sheep. This

---

46   Michael Frost, *Seeing God in the Ordinary*, (Michigan, Baker Books, 2000), 41.

story is undoubtedly disturbing at many levels, not least the destiny of those who do not look out for the vulnerable and hurting in our communities. Yet in all of the parables, there is no forceful demanding or judgemental approach. In the religious culture that is my background and home, there has at times been a harshness in how the wonder of God's amazing grace has been presented that is alien to the storytelling Jesus. "And that, perhaps, is the greatest genius of the parable: it doesn't grab you by the lapels and scream in your face, 'Repent, you vile sinner! Turn or burn!' Rather, it works gently, subtly, indirectly. It respects your dignity. It doesn't batter you into submission but leaves you free to discover and choose for yourself."[47]

As I am reflecting on the Jesus that I am seeking to follow, there are still some hard questions for someone in the position of church oversight to which I have been called. How do these thoughts on the storytelling of Jesus disturb and encourage me in my discipleship and ministry that flows from that discipleship? "When we preach sermons, or hand on ready-made summaries of Christian belief and theology, we inevitably present ourselves as experts. Doing it that way, it is all but impossible to avoid giving the impression that we are people who have it all together, people with no questions. But when we tell stories, we reveal ourselves as weak and vulnerable - spiritual pilgrims with whom others can identify."[48] I find in the storytelling of Jesus room for my struggling and questioning, space to grow and affirmation of how my humanity finds a home in the eternal and amazing grace made known in this Jesus. The father runs toward the wayward son to welcome him home once the son has the courage to recognise his vulnerability and brokenness. In our preaching and teaching, we are not experts but fellow-disciples revelling in the awesome love of a God who is beyond my comprehension but of whom, I get glimpses in human form, in this jewel in the mess, that is Jesus.

The church of today is also facing a crisis of declining numbers

---

47   Brian McLaren, *The Secret Message of Jesus*, (Tennessee, Thomas Nelson, 2006), 48.

48   Riddell, *Threshold of the Future*, 155.

and the traditional expressions of church are finding it increasingly difficult to connect with people in local communities. There is a danger that we suddenly talk about being more missional without working out what that implies. The church today has to be clearly missional focused, as that is the essence of our calling to go into the world baptising and making disciples. However, I want to learn again from this incredible and exciting moment of incarnation. Jesus came into the mess of the world and did not fix the mess, but somehow by his extraordinary life, teaching, death and resurrection, he brought a new beginning to all. We as fellow-disciples have to find ways of being in the mess and confusion of the world and not seek to fix it or save it, but to be Jesus in each and every local community. Our calling is to be like him and somehow together to live his life in the mess.

This birth is like no other and, like Mary, we are to ponder on these events and learn again and again how they can change our lives as individuals and as faith communities. 'The ministry of Mary - being alongside the Christ child, both caring in the midst of vulnerability and standing in awe of divinity, anxious that one is unworthy to be so close to, so trusted with, so touched by the mystery, and yet realising that somehow, in ways beyond one's own desiring, deserving, or comprehending, one has brought forth the fruit of the Spirit and beheld its glory.'[12]

It is the ordinariness of this birth that causes us difficulty. From our perspective, we assume that God's arrival on earth ought to be accompanied by the kind of strange goings-on that we expect in nativity plays: cows that never poop, a baby that never cries, wise men's camels parked in the stable. The one thing we can't bear for Jesus to be is ordinary, for his ordinariness invites us to follow him by providing us with a template of how to be Godlike even as an ordinary human being.'[13] I believe we need to rediscover the simplicity, ordinariness and vulnerability of this moment, so we can be in awe at how God has made known his amazing grace in a tiny, helpless and crying baby.

If these events were to unfold today, you could imagine the world's media being present. There would be telephoto lenses and there would be little privacy, as we would want everyone to know how amazing this moment is. Yet this is not the way God planned the birth of Jesus. It happened in a way very few people would know about, although Bethlehem is now famous and much visited by pilgrims. The words of the Christmas Carol sum up the wonder of this moment:

> 'How silently, How silently,
> The wondrous gift is given,
> When God imparts to human hearts,
> The wonders of His heaven.'[14]

---

12 Samuel Wells, *Incarnational Ministry* (Norwich, Canterbury Press, 2017), 113.
13 Frost, *Exiles*, 37.
14 A verse of the hymn 'O Little Town of Bethlehem' by Phillips Brooks.

CHAPTER 7

ENCOUNTERS

As part of my sabbatical, I went on a pilgrimage to Iona and also spent a few days on Mull, where we were joined by our daughter, Ruth, and son-in-law, Matthew. We have spent time in both these delightful places before and enjoy the pace of life and the incredibly beautiful scenery, beaches, ferry crossings and the single track roads (mostly if not always)! There is a definitive awareness of being away from the busyness and restless activity of everyday life. We enjoyed worship in the Abbey and the hospitality of people on both Iona and Mull.

While we were on Iona, our daughter had a serious accident on Mull while cycling and was transported by ambulance to Craignure accident and emergency. She had come off her bike on the road to Calgary beach and had landed on her face, sustaining a deep cut. We quickly left Iona and travelled to the hospital. Matthew had called us and told us about what had happened and we were concerned. We learnt about the many people who had helped them at the time. A girl who worked in the local cafe in Calgary, who had left her studies as a medical student, was magnificent until the ambulance came. She hopes to become a paramedic and I hope her dreams are fulfilled, as she will be a gift to so many in years to come. The paramedics who arrived in the ambulance, one is close to retirement, the other the only female paramedic on the island, were both very reassuring. The hospital staff of nurses and local general practitioner all did what they do everyday, but with such care and compassion. She was transferred to Glasgow by helicopter for surgery and was given such amazing care by all. We met the pilot of the helicopter who had family roots in Northern Ireland. The paramedics who travelled with her in the air ambulance gave such reassurance and help.

Ruth and Matthew showed such appreciation at a very stressful time. They and we are very grateful to the ordinary and yet special people who showed such kindness and care at that anxious moment. The following is from the delightful book *Wonder*: "If every single person in this room made it a rule that wherever you are, whenever you can, you will try to act a little kinder than is necessary - the world really would be a better place. And if you do this, if you act just a little kinder than is necessary, someone else, somewhere, someday, may recognise in you, the face of God."[49]

These acts of human kindness and understanding of people underpin the encounters, as recorded in the gospel narratives, with Jesus and those in need and pain. It is his ability to offer compassion to those with whom he interacts that make these moments so beautiful and life changing. He sees each person as made in the image of God. They are unique and special. He does not see them as people to fix but as individuals who need to experience the life-changing wonder of encounter with God in human form - to meet grace face to face and never to be the same again.

The speed and urgency of Mark's gospel narrative is something I have always enjoyed and it is all the more obvious when you can read this gospel as a single unit. "There is an air of breathless excitement in nearly every sentence he writes. The sooner we get the message, the better off we'll be, for the message is good, incredibly good: God is here, and he's on our side." (MSG) From the beginning of this ministry that Jesus exercised, there was astonishment and crowds were drawn to hear him and to find healing. His presence changed lives. The man with the unclean spirit was freed from the nightmare of his life. This was the beginning of a ministry of healing and blessing, which Mark records just after Jesus had called the first disciples. Jesus had come to bless people in the mess of their lives and Mark's account of ministry begins in the chaos of this moment. The crowds quickly recognise something special is happening and they flock to him. There is a quiet, gentle and yet resolute authority in how Jesus brings healing,

49   R.J. Palacio, *Wonder* (New York, Penguin, 2017), 301.

release and hope. These miracles are signs of the kingdom of God present in the confusion, pain and struggle of everyday life for those he touched with healing and peace.

Mark then records the healing of a leper. This happens after Jesus has gone off in the middle of the night to pray. The crowds were following him and demanding to see and hear him. The man with leprosy asks a very unusual question that draws a moving response from Jesus. "It is not the standard request for help, but a genuine uncertainty about whether anyone could believe he deserved it, and we are told the words moved Jesus."[50] The response from Jesus was to touch him, a deep expression of caring humanity. "His action expresses compassion."[51] Jesus shows empathy and understanding of the distress and hurt in this person who did not consider himself worthy of help. There is something deeply human and reassuring in touch, especially with those who are in pain or who have such low self-esteem.

There are two levels at which I find this encounter encouraging. First, in my own personal journey of self-discovery, I have only recently recognised that I have lived much of my adult life believing that 'I am not good enough'. In spending time with cognitive therapy because of experiencing some difficult and dark moments with depression, it has become clear that my childhood left me with a sense of vulnerability and of always doubting myself. This has left me over-compensating and trying very hard to prove myself, which is exhausting, and I have had to spend time realising that I have believed that I am not good enough. I do not need to compare myself with others or feel inferior to them. I am a child of God whom Jesus values and indeed cherishes and he will always offer compassion and grace to me. Second, I find it affirming that Jesus sees very clearly the pain and hurt in this leper, who remains nameless, and yet who offers insight into how Jesus understands the mess of people's lives and offers compassion and hope. I have heard so many people express their hurt at how the church has

---

50   Williams, *Lectionary Reflections Year B*, 33.
51   C.E.B. Cranfield, St Mark - *The Cambridge Greek New Testament Commentary*, (Cambridge, Cambridge University Press, reprint 1983), 93.

failed to understand their struggle and instead has offered them platitudes and judgement. We have the responsibility to find ways of showing Jesus as the one who comes alongside the mess of people's lives and brings blessing and hope. The following quote appears harsh and yet it is worth noting, as I believe we, as disciples today, need to respond to it. "Frequently our churches are empty not because the Christian faith is unacceptable to the modern world, but because of the 'counter-witness of believers and Christian communities failing to follow the model of Christ.'(Redemptoris Missio 36). In many respects our track record is against us."[52] We need to find ways of incarnating the loveliness of Jesus into the mess and hurt of our local communities.

The man was instructed not to tell anyone, which was impossible now that his life was restored to him. Jesus did instruct him to ensure that he should go through the official system to have the stigma of leprosy removed from his life and thanks be given to God in the temple. The one sure and certain thing is that this man's life, having had such a beautiful encounter with Jesus, would never be the same again!

It is fascinating that reading scripture can continually give new insights and possibilities, for example when reading the passages where Jesus forgives and heals the paralysed man. "Most people don't realise that this was probably Jesus' own house. Jesus was the unlucky householder that had his roof ruined that day. This opens up quite a new possibility for understanding what Jesus said to the paralysed man. How would you feel if someone made a big hole in your roof? But Jesus looks down and says, with a rueful smile: 'All right I forgive you!' Something in his voice though, made them realise this was different. Jesus was speaking with a quiet authority that went down into the paralysed man's innermost being. Only the priests could declare forgiveness, speaking in the name of God. If that's what this man needed, his friends should take him to the temple in Jerusalem, not to a wandering preacher."[53] This is yet another delightful encounter and there are issues raised at this moment that Mark will

---

52 David J. Bosch, *Believing in the Future*, (Herefordshire, Gracewing, 1995), 45.

53 Wright, *Mark for Everyone*, 16-17.

return to in his gospel account: the question of forgiveness and who can forgive sins. The reference to the 'son of man' gives clear echoes of Daniel and the representative of God's people will be vindicated by God and he will be given authority to forgive sins. These are thoughts for a later chapter but for now, the human encounter is one of a man who could not walk being healed and enabled to walk.

There is one aspect of this event that has always fascinated me and that is that this man had four friends who cared enough to carry him to Jesus. Over many years in pastoral ministry, I have met many such friends who cared enough to pray and care for those in need. Their friendship was such a special gift to those in need. Part of our personal discipleship is to care for one another and to bring each other to Jesus. This may be in acts of kindness, service or prayer. It is in the ordinary expressions of care that we can make such a difference to others.

There are two more encounters I want to reflect upon but Mark beautifully weaves them together. Jesus receives an urgent request from Jairus regarding his very ill daughter. However, Jesus is inter-rupted on his way to see her, when a woman who has been suffer-ing from a blood disorder touches him. There are similarities and yet profound differences between these two encounters. Jairus and the unnamed woman are driven by fear and panic. Every parent can iden-tify with Jairus and his fear concerning his girl. As a parent I know we would do anything to protect our children from sickness and pain, you would rather take their place. This fear can numb and strangle you as your hopes and fears pull in different directions. Jairus, a dis-tinguished member of the local community, puts himself at the mercy of Jesus by kneeling at his feet and begging for help. Jesus went with him and was, as always, followed by the crowds.

This encounter is then paused as we meet the woman who has had internal bleeding for 12 years. She is desperate and fearful. She has spent all her wealth on possible treatments and is now placing all her hopes on touching Jesus. This distressed woman does not want to be noticed or discovered as she is ashamed of her condition and it would bring her further disgrace. As Mark records this account there is a moment of awe as she touches his garment and Jesus notices that power has left him. The disciples mock his response as the crowds were crushing him, everyone is touching him! Then the woman meets Jesus and there is a liberating moment when she knows she is healed and her faith and courage have been acknowledged. I do envy the disciples who witnessed these encounters as they must have noticed the eye contact, the holiness of the life-changing moments, when lives were turned upside down.

The element of touch in many of the encounters Jesus had with people intrigues me and there is something about touch that appears to affirm and envelope people in hope. "Healing by touch, not least when the healer wasn't expecting it, is such a strange phenomenon that we probably can't probe much further about how such things work. But they highlight for us the intimate nature of the contact between the individual and Jesus that Mark expects and hopes the reader to develop for themselves. When life crowds in with all its pressures, there is still room for us to creep up behind Jesus - if that's all we feel we can do - and reach out to touch him, in that old mixture of fear and faith that characterises so much Christian discipleship."[54]

We then return to the devastating news that Jairus' daughter has died. This is a nightmare for this distraught parent. I have tragically witnessed that horrendous moment when a parent discovers their child is dead. There are no words that can help their distress and trite religious clichés only insult the pain. Jesus goes with him to his house and people laughed at him because he told them she was only sleeping. He instructed her to get up and she did, much to the amazement of many and, I dare say, the confusion of some. There are deeper issues being set out by Mark in this account that he will return to as Jesus faces his own death and resurrection. There was a deeper revolution of God's kingdom taking place and in time that will be revealed.

When I read this and other encounters, I wonder about the many people Jesus didn't heal, the many children who died when he was

---

54   Wright, *Mark for Everyone*, 60-1.

travelling around the countryside and who were not raised to life. Jesus came into the mess and brought blessing, healing and hope, but he did not take away the hurt and pain of the world. However, I want to find in these encounters pointers that can help me and fellow-disciples today to live in the mess of the world and live out the presence of Jesus by our life together as fellow-disciples.

Jesus was always available, approachable, receptive to help others and graceful. He was where the people were and those in need flocked to him to find these grace-filled encounters. May we as local Christian communities seek to be Jesus to all in our communities and may they find us approachable and graceful.

> Which takes us to the dusty, messy, bloody and
> unexpected stories about Jesus,
> who
> touches lepers, whom no one else would touch,
> and
> hears the cry of blind people, who had been told to be
> quiet,
> and
> dines with tax collectors, whom everybody hated,
> and
> talks with thirsty, loose Samaritan women he wasn't
> supposed to talk with -
> over and over again we see him going to the edges, to
> the margins, to those in trouble, those despised, those no
> one else would touch, those who were ignored, the weak,
> the blind, the lame, the lost, the losers.
>
> He moves toward them;
> he extends himself to them;
> he reaches out to them;
> he meets them in their place of pain, helplessness,
> abandonment, and failure.

He is living, breathing evidence that God wants everybody, everyone, to be rescued, renewed, and reconciled to ourselves, our neighbours, our world, and God.[55]

---

55   Rob Bell, *What We Talk About When We Talk About God*, (New York, HarperCollins, 2014), 141-2.

CHAPTER 8

GRACE MOMENTS

It was one of those scenes that will disturb and shape me for the rest of my life. It was formative in so many ways, not least as it asked serious questions of faith in an overtly religious society and culture. The tensions of that day are still evident in the country that is home for me and a country I love. Growing up in Northern Ireland, with the many symbols of faith and identity, shaped and moulded my faith, but it also forced me to struggle with faith as it has often been portrayed. It was through my own experiences of living in a fractured community that I had to wrestle with my own understanding of faith. There was a very clear recognition on my part that if I was seeking to follow Jesus, the call to reconciliation and bridge-building was inescapable. Too often symbols, words and elements of the faith community were divisive and, from my perspective, lacking in grace. They would have said and perhaps still would say that they were standing for truth. This was something which has played a huge part in my journey of faith lived out in ordained ministry in the place I call home.

When this incident happened, I was a young teenager. It was late at night and our family home was on the Woodstock Road, a main road out of the city going east. The house was opposite a police station or Willowfield Barracks as it was called. On the one side of the station was my parish church, Willowfield parish, now a thriving church in the heart of the community and finding ways to bless people in the mess. On the other side was St Anthony's chapel, the local Roman Catholic parish. There was also a nunnery and the priest's house nearby. This occurred during what was a tense period of the Troubles, when there were various riots and attacks on police and other facilities, particularly in loyalist and republican communities in the early 1970s. This evening, the riot started when a crowd gathered. It was terrifying watching how quickly the crowd became a very angry mob vying for blood. There were rioters in our small front garden, which had no soil or plants, just concrete and a brick wall. They were trying to get pieces of brick and concrete. The police station was attacked and then the chapel was desecrated, with confession boxes destroyed and various statues broken. The priest locked himself in the upper part of the house and but for the army arriving, it could have been a tragic ending. "The name of Jesus, whose life and message resonated with acceptance, welcome and inclusion, has too often become a symbol of elitism, exclusion and aggression."[56] The people who caused this mayhem were probably not church-goers and might have struggled with faith but they were acting in the name of Protestantism and attacking a Catholic Church. This use and abuse of religion and religious language constantly disturbed my early years of faith. There are times today when I find myself disturbed at how religious differences can still cause very aggressive reactions.

I was shocked and frightened that night and it left me with many questions, struggling to find ways of holding together my faith in Jesus and what was described as a religious war. One of the issues that I always find difficult is the one of self-righteousness, when religious people try to justify their actions by the sinfulness of others. When we compare ourselves with others, we can feel so good about ourselves or at least we think we can. "Unlike the sins that are commonly noticed and repented of by a worshipping congregation, self-righteousness is almost never recognised in the mirror. Occasionally in someone else, never in me."[57]

That was a formative moment in my faith journey, as it helped me grapple with some of the unwritten codes of behaviour in my community - the mentality of a 'them and us', of a religiously divided community. This polarisation was often hidden behind various code

---

56   Brian McLaren, *A Generous Orthodoxy*, (Michigan, Zondervan, 2006), 71.

57   Peterson, *Tell it Slant*, 88.

phrases such as "they are a nice person but..." or "I am not sure you can trust them because...." There is no doubt there was and still is much sectarianism in my community and this is something that is still being addressed. There are also deep hurts and somehow we have to find ways of dealing with the past if we are not to be enslaved by them. We have to find grace to recognise the hurt we have caused each other and how a lack of grace has damaged the future possibilities. There is a particular need among those of us who seek to follow Jesus to learn to be a blessing in the mess and of finding ways of recognising the Jesus in each other and how together we present a more rounded and beautiful image of the word made flesh.

I want to recognise the people who have helped me on this journey in my episcopal friends, Bishop Noel Treanor, Bishop Tony Farquhar and Bishop Donal McKeown, who have affirmed me and given me the gift of encouragement. From my days in parish life, I am grateful for the friendship of Fr Gerry Patton, the best storyteller I have ever met. The hospitality and prayers of the Benedictine brothers in Holy Cross Monastery in Rostrevor, have been an amazing gift to me in times of retreat and renewal. These and many others from traditions other than my own have helped me find Jesus in the other, in the mess of the tortured and beautiful community of Northern Ireland.

Reflecting on the angry crowd and the religious self-righteousness makes me turn to one of the scenes described in John's gospel: the angry religious group who came to Jesus, making a woman caught in the act of adultery stand in front of Jesus and the crowd who were gathered to listen to him. There are difficulties with this text in terms of where it should be. However, in the words of Tom Wright: "There is a puzzle about this story. It doesn't really seem to fit here. And, tellingly the earliest copies of John's gospel do in fact run straight from 7.52 to 8.12, missing the story out altogether. At the same time, some manuscripts put it in, but in a different place. Some even place it in Luke's gospel (and it has to be said that the way the story is told is, if anything, more like Luke than like John)... At the same time there is something to be said for reading it here, where a lot of manuscripts do have it."[58]

The woman caught in the act of adultery was being used by those who wanted to trap Jesus. It is strange and yet culturally correct that the woman was the one in the firing line of the crowd. There would have been a man guilty of the same sin and yet he is not pursued as guilty. They were enjoying the fact that they were better than her and, in so doing, humiliating her. But they believed they had trapped Jesus. If he said her sins were forgiven then he would be teaching them to forget about the teaching in the law of Moses. His answer was something I find amazing - the speed of thought, the ability to answer and yet say much more than they would have expected. This is wisdom and grace mingled together in sheer beauty. There are many words written about what Jesus was writing in the sand but I am not sure it matters. Perhaps he was trying to take the attention away from the frightened woman or perhaps he was biding for time. It is fun to speculate, but the answer is what changed the scene dramatically.

The ultimate recognition is made that nobody is without sin and therefore nobody could throw the first stone. Self-righteousness disappears when we recognise our own brokenness. We no longer judge ourselves by others but by the truth that we all fall short of the glory of God. The law is not a weapon to help us judge ourselves against others but to enable us to recognise our own need of grace and mercy. It must be said that Jesus does not condone adultery and the women is offered forgiveness; in fact, her life has been given back to her. She was facing stoning from an angry crowd. Her sin is forgiven by God's mercy and the words of Jesus are clear: "Neither do I condemn you. Go your way, and from now on do not sin again."[59]

I am intrigued by these words of Jesus and it depends in what tone they are said. Was it a scolding sense of now go and don't do this again or else? Was it a grace moment that recognised the pain and hurt of her life and offered her the grace to live differently and, in

---

58   Wright, *John for Everyone*, 111.
59   John 8:11 NRSV.

that sense, it was a statement of hope and new beginnings? My view is that it was the latter, a beautiful moment when Jesus, in the mess of someone's life, blessed them and enabled them to begin again in the mess, as her life was the same and yet it would never be the same again. "The use of the present continuous here is a challenge to her, and to us, to lead a new life."[60]

From my own childhood, I witnessed the harshness there can be to judge others in the context of a community of faith. This judgement and self-righteousness are unattractive and cause much pain in those who are seen as not worthy. A gambling husband left my dear mum alone with two sons, homeless and penniless. My grandparents and my mum's family were amazing and showed such grace and love. However, my mum found the church a difficult place because she was now a separated lady, even though my father, through the dreadful disease of being a gambling addict, left her without a home, or money, and with two young boys to raise. I am biased and I believe she did an amazing job and the wider family circle made our lives secure and surrounded us with love. However, some members of the local church found it difficult not to treat her differently and she at times felt uncomfortable. To her amazing credit, when I offered myself for selection for ordination she was very supportive. Ironically, I was ordained and have spent my life serving the church that caused her pain. There is no doubt that her experience has helped me cope and understand the brokenness of the people, who are the church, I am called to serve and represent. Her faith in Jesus did not waiver, but remained strong, although quiet and unassuming.

The focus here must be on Jesus who, in the brokenness of people's lives, gave hope and new beginnings, not fixing the mess, but enabling people to live in it differently. "Jesus had the uncanny ability to look at everyone with grace filled eyes, seeing not only the beauty of who they were but also the sacred potential of what they could become. We his followers have the same challenge: 'So from now on we regard no one from a worldly point of view,' Paul told the

60 Burridge, John: *The People's Bible Commentary*, 111.

Corinthians. Evidently we are not doing likewise since many people think of faith, especially evangelical faith as bad news. They believe Christians view them through eyes of judgement, not eyes of grace."[61]

Many years ago, I was given a nickname by my children which has stuck. I am known to my children as 'Big Al' or 'Big Man' and, occasionally since being ordained a bishop, 'Big Purple'. The important word in any of these is 'Big'; as someone who is five foot seven, there is a certain irony to this name. It is important to admit that I used to be very sensitive about being small and was very disappointed when, at the age of 18, I was refused entry into the police as I was an inch too small.

It is therefore no surprise that one of my favourite characters in the gospel accounts is Zacchaeus. Luke is the only gospel record of this small man who also happened to be a chief tax collector. "Luke's is the only gospel that tells of him and his sudden moment of glory, and the hardened tax-collector fits in to three of Luke's regular themes: the problem of riches and what to do about it, the identification of Jesus with 'sinners', and the faith which recognises Jesus as Lord and discovers new life as a result."[62] This account of Zacchaeus in Luke's record follows soon after the encounter between Jesus and the rich young ruler. The encounter with the rich young ruler leaves us with an unfinished record. What happened to him? Did he sell his goods and give to the poor? As I read the many encounters in the gospels between various people and Jesus, this young man is the only one who leaves Jesus not feeling better about himself, apart from the various self-righteous people who were trying to catch Jesus out on so many occasions.

However, the meeting with Zacchaeus is a delightful moment when we see Jesus yet again doing the radical thing and eating with 'sinners'. He is determined to model this risk-taking of leaving the safe religious world of his day and seeking to be where people are. In the mess and ordinariness of their lives, he is present and thereby

---

61   Philip Yancey, *Vanishing Grace,* (London, Hodder and Stoughton, 2014), 55.

62   Wright, *Luke for Everyone,* 222.

gains the opportunity to bring grace and offer new beginnings. "Jesus knew how to occupy the third spaces of his culture, and always operated in a setting where he would naturally bump into people."[63]

This is a challenge for the parish structure and context in which I am called to exercise oversight. Many of our faithful and committed people are so busy and exhausted keeping the parish structure afloat that there is little energy or time left for engaging with people in their community. There is also the danger that many people who commute to where they worship have little contact with people who live in the area of the parish. Too few people are doing too much in local parish communities and thereby they have no time for building friendship and connection with those who find church difficult. We have also tended to operate with the philosophy that you have to believe before you can belong to the church. These are issues we have to struggle with and find ways of being creative and imaginative. I am increasingly convinced that in today's culture people need to belong before they will believe and we have to find ways of recognising this. We need more and more grace moments where people encounter Jesus when they encounter us. In the midst of these struggles and questions, I am also convinced that there are signs of the kingdom at work in local communities that are looking for something beyond themselves. "God is up to something in our neighbourhoods, on the ground in real places. The church, in all its diversity, needs to figure out how to join in."[64]

In these encounters, I find the most striking element is the way that Jesus so naturally and freely dispenses grace. There are no strings attached and people are accepted as they are with the grace potential to rediscover the beautiful image of God already deep within them. This is a grace that transforms and radiates hope and potential. "When it comes to engaging others we don't have to wonder what Jesus would have done. The Bible's really clear about telling us

63   John Drane, *After McDonaldization*, (London, DLT, 2008), 57.
64   Paul Sparks, Tim Soerens and Dwight J. Friesen, *The New Parish*, (Illinois, InterVarsity Press, 2014), 77.

over and over again, exactly what he did do when engaging others. He loved them. He didn't assess their worth, or evaluate their moral standing, or in any way determine their quality before he loved them. He 'simply' loved and respected them, exactly as they were."[65]

One of the key aspects of this as I seek to find ways of following Jesus is to view and react to everyone I encounter as made in the image of God. "There is no one, and surely no entire people, in whom the image of God has been utterly extinguished. Faith in God means believing that anyone can be transformed, regardless of the past."[66] I pray that the Holy Spirit will give us the ability to see people as Jesus does, with the eyes of God and thereby made in his image. However, I must confess that this is much more difficult in practice. This is something that must become a discipline and a conscious decision. It is much easier to judge and assess others than it is to see them as made in the image of God, but we have the example and witness of Jesus to challenge and inspire us.

In the future of how we will exercise our communal life in parish and local church, we will have to find new ways of doing this. The present parish structure as I am experiencing it, is struggling with financial difficulties, the maintaining of buildings and the continuity of ministry. With these pressing issues, it is all the more difficult to engage with people who do not connect with faith as represented by the church. How can we help people to tell their life stories and somehow see how they can be part of God's story and how they are of amazing value to him? "Notwithstanding statements to the contrary, many churches find it difficult to offer a space in which people can actually reflect on their personal stories in a way that enables them to see God at work."[67]

I believe that as we seek to incarnate Jesus in our broken communities with so many people looking for something beyond their experience we will have to do church differently. It will require a

65   John Shore, *I'm OK - You're Not*, (Colorado, NavPress, 2007), 122.

66   Walter Wink, *The Powers that Be*, (New York, Doubleday, 1998), 178.

67   Drane, *After McDonaldization*, 113.

radical rethink of the use of our buildings, finance and ministry. This is a very real challenge, but I also believe it is a wonderful God-given opportunity. It never ceases to amaze me when I take time to listen to people how many stories there are of people who have found church a difficult place but who long to be heard and valued. So often we fail to hear these stories because we never take the time or we are too busy doing things for others rather than being with them by our listening presence. This is our calling to be Jesus for and with others and by enabling them to rediscover the image of God within.

CHAPTER 9

RELIGIOSITY

I am very grateful for the many people who influenced me and helped shape me on my journey of faith. My early faith journey was a struggle of trying to make sense of Jesus in what was a strange religious world where fear and guilt were dominant features. There was a fear of somehow not being true to some objective truth that was always right. There was also guilt at questioning or probing some of these issues. As I reflect back upon my early years in adult faith, I can now see that I was more concerned about others approving of me than of me being willing to take risks for Jesus. In this religious world, there was a critical need to conform to the group belief system. All churches and faith communities have this element of control and with my personality this was difficult. I have always liked the grey areas of faith, the desire to probe and not just accept things.

"In his book *The Great Awakening*, Jim Wallis describes how as a young man growing up in evangelical church, he never heard a sermon on the Sermon on the Mount. All that the preacher ever talked about were the salvation passages from John and Paul. Think how very different the gospel sounds when one sings Mary's radical song, 'The Magnificat'. It's no wonder the body of Christ is splintered into a thousand pieces. Like those blindfolded children and the 'piñata' everyone claims a different piece of Jesus, and then, in separate rooms, they gorge themselves on it."[68] I can identify with this experience when my own faith has been challenged and stretched as I have discovered wonderful facets of God's amazing grace through many different people whose background and faith community are

68   Robin Meyers, *The Underground Church*, (London, S.P.C.K., 2011), 20-1. Reproduced with permission of the Licensor through PLSclear.

very different from mine. It has been a particular privilege to be involved in the World Council of Churches and to hear and experience different worship styles and understandings of being a disciple in different cultures and contexts. There is such joy in being able to see new dimensions of Jesus as revealed by other traditions and individuals. In my own early faith journey, the critical issue was personal salvation and there was little acknowledgement of how I could grow as a disciple and of how we were meant to incarnate the presence of Jesus in local communities.

There was a 'them' and 'us' mentality of those who belonged and those who most certainly didn't. It was at times harsh and unattractive. The main issue was to ensure people were safe for eternity. The question of eternity is important, but I believe that the message was, and is, lost if there is no lifestyle that radiates the message better than words and gives integrity and reality to the joy and struggle of following Jesus.

In my own journey, it was at times difficult to see where was the place of struggle or doubt. My experience was that it was those who were absolutely certain and definite on all these matters of personal faith that I found most difficult and that is still true today. There is no place for mystery and uncertainty. They appear to have a hot-line to heaven and my struggle was, and is, testimony to my supposed lack of faith. "Thus first, our message is that whoever you are, whatever you are struggling with, whatever your doubts, questions and temptations, God understands the difficulties you are facing and has faced them himself. Then we go on to say that we struggle too, that we don't have all the answers. Life is also a battle for us. We have fears and insecurities, temptations and unanswered questions."[69]

There was little sense of Christian community that was meant to live out this glorious message of grace. Individualism was a strong emphasis that meant there was little or no ecclesiology. In fact, there was suspicion and mistrust of institutional church. There needs to

69   Steve Chalke, *Intelligent Church*, (Michigan, Zondervan, 2006), 74.

be a recognition that this is God's mission and the church is meant to be a servant to this mission. "Many churches, particularly those driven by church growth models, come dangerously close to reducing Christianity to a commodity that can be packaged, marketed and sold. Instead of cultivating a deep, holistic discipleship that touches every aspect of our lives, we've confined the life of faith to Sunday mornings, where it can be kept safe and predictable, or to a 'personal relationship with Jesus Christ,' which can be managed from the privacy of our own home. Following Jesus has been diminished to a privatised faith rather than a lifelong apprenticeship undertaken in the context of Christian community."[70]

We are called to community as fellow-disciples and it is in our love for one another and the stranger that we can incarnate and be the presence of Jesus. We are a sacrament of presence in the pain and loneliness of the present-day culture. "In the midst of all the violence and corruption of the world God invites us today to create new places of belonging, places of sharing, of peace and kindness, places where no-one needs to defend himself or herself; places where each one is loved and accepted with one's own fragility, abilities and disabilities. This is my vision for our churches: that they become places of belonging, places of sharing."[71]

Throughout the gospel narratives, there is the constant thread of the religious people struggling with Jesus. This is very understandable, as he was so different and exciting, appealing to the crowds and saying and doing some bewildering things. In fact, it is important to recognise that the disciples were not aware of the enormity of what Jesus was doing until after the resurrection. They were following, but there were different occasions when they were not on the same page as Jesus. Their confusion, misunderstanding and humanity are very refreshing for fellow-disciples today. Jesus' harshest criticism was for the religious people, who were hypocritical, using their religion to

---

70   C. Christopher Smith and John Pattison, *Slow Church*, (Illinois, InterVarsity Press, 2014), 14.

71   Jean Vanier, *Befriending the Stranger*, (New Jersey, Paulist Press, 2010), 12.

further their own ends or make themselves look better than others and thereby judging others.

Luke records the story of the two men going up to the temple to pray. "One of the theological tasks of our day is to learn how to tell the parable of the two men in the Temple so that it shocks and surprises our world as Jesus' story did his, opening up a vision of God's justice which is not fooled by possessions and prestige, or by social standing, but sees to the heart, and hears the genuine cry of the sinner."[72] Yet again the stories that Jesus tells make us look at the world through different lens. The religious man is doing all the right things in terms of living out his faith and all are very commendable things, but he is comparing himself with the tax collector. The introduction to the story tells us that it is for those who think of themselves as better than others.

Increasingly, as I reflect upon the religious role that I inhabit, this is such an important issue. Those of us who seek to follow Jesus can easily give the impression that we have everything sorted, that we are very together people and can make ourselves feel good as we compare ourselves with others. This is very unattractive and actually in the context of this story very dangerous. As I understand the essence of personal discipleship, it is my brokenness and vulnerability that are my greatest gifts in discovering God's kingdom within. "For as long as we hold on to any pretence of having it all together we are prevented from deepening and maturing in the Christian faith. For as long as we avoid recognition of our lostness we are prevented from experiencing the elegant profundities of foundness."[73]

In the religious world of church and culture in which I seek to live out my discipleship there has long been the danger of self-righteousness and lack of compassion for those who do not belong. The roles we perform in church life or society do not make us better than anyone else. In fact they can often hide the deep brokenness within us as we can be busy playing at religion. I speak

72   Tom Wright, *Twelve Months of Sundays: Year C*, (London, S.P.C.K., 2000), 117.
73   Peterson, *Tell it Slant*, 98.

of my own experience of listening to many, where harsh words of judgement have caused much pain to those who are genuinely trying to make sense of their broken lives but find little grace to help. We have to recognise that the world of church can be a difficult place for those who do not belong. How do we become less religious and self-righteous, instead being transformative by being grace dispensers? As part of this rediscovery there has to be an honest recognition that we as the church have much to do to rebuild trust and integrity with many people. The religious world we inherit can hide us from some difficult truths. "To many outside the church, 'Church' is what some others do. It is noticed sadly, in their terms, not only as an alien and expensive building that I wouldn't know what to do in; worse, it is occupied by people I wouldn't be seen dead with. To them, church stands for internal bickering over issues no one else cares about, inconsistent lives that makes claims in words ridiculous, led by people who don't know what they believe and are probably to be distrusted with other people's children."[74] These are harsh words, but we need to recognise how we have failed to be bearers of Christ's image and recognise our failure and brokenness. God's greatest gift to us is the recognition of our failure and the grace to try again. Underpinning this is the belief that must be a core value for us and that is that the church is primarily for those who do not belong. "The Church is the Church only when it exists for others."[75]

Many years ago, I was persuaded by our parish organist to take the lead role in the musical *Godspell*. Ian was very persuasive and a very talented musical director and this show led to many more shows where people discovered hidden talents for singing, dancing and acting. I never quite got the dancing. There are two particular songs that I remember as they captured such raw emotion. They were 'On The

74   George Lings, *Encounters on the Edge - Living Proof*, (Sheffield, The Sheffield Centre, Church Army, 1999), 13-14.
75   Dietrich Bonhoeffer, *Letters and Papers from Prison*, (New York, MacMillan, 1967), 203-4.

Willows' and 'Alas for You'. The first of these was sung during the emotional scene when Jesus was saying farewell to the disciples in the moments before his betrayal. We had agreed under Ian's creative direction to find an individual way for each disciple to say goodbye. All of us found this scene deeply moving every time we performed it; there was a profound sadness which was more than acting, and we in our own hearts, minds and spirits felt we experienced something of the mystery of what had happened in the gospel narrative.

'Alas for You' was a song that I found difficult to sing because of the words, the tempo and the music. What was even harder was capturing the anger and frustration that was in these words. Jesus was very angry at the abuse of religion. The script of *Godspell* is based on the account of Matthew's gospel and these words are based on the accounts of Matthew 23:13-33. "Basically he accuses them of getting things the wrong way around. They are valuing gold above the Temple, and the gifts above the altar. They are placing higher worth on objects that human beings have brought into God's presence than on God's presence itself... They are guilty of breaking the third commandment. And they are covering up with slick arguments about what counts and what doesn't."[76] Before making any further comment on these encounters it is important to add the following; "It's true that Matthew's gospel, not least this chapter, has sometimes been used as a weapon in anti-Jewish or anti-Semitic, propaganda. But this is a flagrant misuse of this text. In Jesus' day, and on to our own day, the great majority of Jews have been, to put it crudely, neither scribes or Pharisees."[77]

At first I had to work really very hard at being angry singing these words not least because singing and acting was very hard work. However, as I grew into this portrayal of the gospel story, I found myself feeling this anger quite deeply. This was real anger at how religious people were using their position to abuse the very religion they were portraying. They were using it to control and manipulate

---

76   Wright, *Matthew for Everyone*, 102.
77   Ibid., 103.

people and to further their own ends. That is very uncomfortable for those of us who live in a religious world. There is no doubt that fear has often been one of the ways that religion has controlled and manipulated people. I grew up fearful of getting it wrong and did not learn until later in my faith journey that following Jesus often meant taking risks with people and for the sake of the kingdom. "It is abusive when people are taught to accept the word of those in authority, and that questioning of that authority is an affront to God."[78] In my own journey, the questions have become more important than the answers because they teach me that I am still learning. The questions also help me wrestle with my faith and that leads to growth and maturity. To deny the opportunity for struggle, questions and doubts removes one of the opportunities for developing. One of the things I have found helpful in my journey is to keep a journal that records the questions and struggles and it can become what I consider to be a personal book of psalms.

The most important lesson that I have learnt in leadership and ministry is that I might not always be right. In fact, being right is not the critical issue but have I behaved with grace and been a grace dispenser? The truth is that I have failed and I recognise with sadness that this is true. Although I take heart from the tax collector that in recognising my failure there is hope for my future. I pray that many more fellow-disciples will recognise the gift of failure and brokenness is the essence of being disciples, not self-righteousness. In penning these thoughts and having had time away from the cut and thrust of ministry and public engagement, I have spent much time in my study/chapel, which is essentially a basement cut off from the rest of our home. I have to leave the house to get to it and can hide there from everything that can disturb and distract; it is my 'cave'. "The idea of a cave in the monastic tradition teaches us that there will be seasons of life, moments in our routine, times of the day, when we need to strip from ourselves all that clutters, comforts and soothes us. We need to go down to the bare rock floor, alone and vulnerable, face

78   Riddell, *Threshold of the Future*, 67-8.

in the dirt, to experience what the ancient Jewish writer of the book of Lamentations experienced:

> "to sit alone in silence
> when the Lord has imposed it,
> to put one's mouth to the dust
> (there may yet be hope)."
> Lamentations 3: 28-29 NRSV[79]

---

79 Adams, *Cave Refectory Road*, 19.

CHAPTER 10

A LEARNER

It is difficult to be sure when my journey of faith started. On reflection, I believe I did try to follow Jesus as a child and teenager, but it really became serious during my last year at school. This was a result of my grandfather dying and my uncertainty about what I was going to do after leaving school. There were many influences along this journey that were key, such as leaders who modelled something of the loveliness of Jesus and a profound sense of Jesus being someone I wanted to follow. In him, there was meaning, purpose and a wonderful sense of acceptance and grace. "Jesus chose his disciples, they did not choose him, for reasons best known to himself; and he accepted them as they were."[80] In reading about the first disciples and how ordinary they were, I find myself greatly encouraged. "The gospels show that Jesus did not select his disciples because they were virtuous or wise. They are often seen squabbling over rank and status, misinterpreting what he said and misunderstanding who he was."[81]

This is very important to emphasise because there is the danger that many people whom I have encountered in parish ministry think that discipleship is only for the very religious and serious person. "It is the very ordinariness of the disciples that gives me hope. Jesus does not seem to choose his followers on the basis of native talent or perfectibility or potential for greatness. I cannot avoid the impression that Jesus prefers working with unpromising recruits."[82] It is the amazing paradox of grace how Jesus takes the ordinary person and calls them to discipleship. One of the joys of this journey with Jesus is the people whom we meet along the way. I am forever grateful

80   Freeman, *Jesus The Teacher Within*, 215.
81   Ibid., 215.
82   Yancey, *The Jesus I Never Knew*, 99-100.

for my dear friend and fellow-disciple, Stanley. We met as students at Queen's University Belfast, and the friendship has survived over four decades. The joy of this friendship is that we can talk about Jesus without embarrassment and with delight. We share our struggles with God, the church and the world. We also share our joys and have been present at important moments of both our family lives. It is the freedom to talk about Jesus that is such a delight. We can say anything and have the space and acceptance to wrestle with issues. This safe space is actually what I describe as a 'holy place' for fellow-disciples. It is where we can nurture and encourage one another as we seek to follow Jesus. I am incredibly thankful for this space because in the strange world of leadership in the church, it is so special to have somewhere where I can be a fellow-disciple. It is vital to have a trusted friend, who knows me well enough, to tell me what I sometimes do not want to hear!

There is also the joy of family who help me know that I am loved and valued, but who also are able to help me laugh at my foibles and idiosyncrasies. I imagine becoming a grandfather will add to those moments of being made to realise my fallibility and humanness. We are never meant to journey with Jesus on our own, but we cannot share our lives with everyone and anyone. We have to find safe places which I want to call 'holy places', because in those moments, I experience the real presence of Jesus. It is in the ordinary moments of being alive that we can find so much of the presence of Jesus. The gifts of friendship, family and life itself can help us recognise his presence with us. I am concerned that we sometimes complicate the simplicity and spontaneity of the spiritual life. "Jesus is a man himself who seems astonished by the ordinary. He regularly refers to the mundane and sees things as indicators of wider truth. He spots lilies in a field, and they remind him of God's care for the human race. For him the innocence of a child's eyes is an indicator of the true humility and awareness after which we should all strive."[83]

Being a disciple is something that is critical to all who seek to

83   Frost, *Seeing God in the Ordinary,* 169.

follow Jesus and it begins with the recognition that it is a calling. "What Jesus says to Peter is, of course, what he says to any who are trying to be his followers. As soon as they can cope with such a thought, even if it challenges them, he says, in effect, 'I am your friend. I offer you the intimacy of friendship. Become, or become more deeply, God's friend'."[84] This is the essence of why I am fascinated by Jesus and I am drawn over and over again to the beauty and wonder, of who he is, and how he deals with people. His constant dispensing of grace, warms my heart and compels me to follow him. For too long in my early years of faith, I was consumed by guilt and fear of getting it wrong, of not pleasing God. However, I have discovered that following Jesus means being free to be who I am, a child of God and cherished by him.

Following Jesus is exciting, demanding, challenging and there are no guarantees or road maps. We are called to follow and somehow by his grace, find ways of reflecting him to others, particularly those who are in the mess of what it can be to be human. I have found this calling to be a disciple has led me to places that I would have preferred not to have experienced: the strange world of ordination where, as I have discovered, it is easy to become detached from the world outside of church. This calling can take over your life, as the institutional church has to struggle and work with the structures of parish and ministry that make mission more difficult today. For clergy the cost can be great and the burden very heavy. "The vicissitudes of life and the demands of ministry can and do grind clergy down."[85]

I have raised the following issue, in a previous chapter, as to how the church has failed in the last century to take part seriously in the aspect of the great commission to make disciples. This is particularly difficult because of the demands in parish life to ensure that every-

84   Michael Perham, *Jesus and Peter*, (London, SPCK, 2012), 47. Reproduced with permission of the Licensor through PLSclear.
85   Jamie Harrison and Robert Innes eds., *Clergy in a Complex Age*, (London, SPCK, 2016), 31.

thing runs as it should. There are too few people doing too many things and clergy are overburdened for there to be any time left, for making disciples. If we are to help incarnate the presence of Jesus, we will have to emphasise discipleship as part of our calling as members of Christ's church. We are all disciples and it is not just for the few. We are all called to be disciples and we are called to be friends with Jesus as we seek to follow him. "Following Jesus means listening intently to what he teaches and trying to live the way he advocates, not picking and choosing the parts of his teaching that appeal and jettisoning those we find difficult or challenging."[86]

Being a disciple is something that I have been trying to do for many years and I find myself still learning; I will never stop learning because a disciple is primarily a learner. "The word disciple derives from *discere*, to learn. A disciple is someone who acknowledges that he has got something to learn."[87] There is a paradox at the heart of my journey that continually encourages me. In my arrogance and naivety in the early years of ministry and discipleship, I thought that I had most, if not all, the answers to the difficult questions people might ask, but, mercifully, I have learnt that I do not, and will not, have those answers. However, I am more and more convinced in the person of Jesus, who continually calls me to follow and to keep learning. My journey of faith, is not about having answers or being able to sort out the mess and pain of others, but it is to know and love him, and somehow by his grace to make him known.

"'Follow me', though was not the only call issued by Jesus to his disciples. There were times when he called people to 'come to me', times when he invited them to 'wait for me', and times when he asked them to 'go for me'. Come, follow, wait, go: each represents a different aspect of the call to discipleship, and each reveals unique facets of the character of Jesus the caller."[88] I have found these elements of discipleship very helpful in seeking to discern how I can best be a disciple in

86 Perham, *Jesus and Peter*, 14.
87 Freeman, *Jesus: The Teacher Within*, 37.
88 Watson, *The Fourfold Leadership of Jesus*, 17-18.

the middle of busyness and constant demands. It has given a structure and a particular discipline to my reflections and praying.

It has been critical at times to hear those words of Jesus recorded by Matthew, with the following translation: "Are you tired? Worn out? Burned out on religion? Come to me. Get away with me and you'll recover your life. I'll show you how to take a real rest. Walk with me and work with me - watch how I do it. Learn the unforced rhythms of grace. I won't lay anything heavy or ill fitting on you. Keep company with me and you'll learn to live freely and lightly." (MSG) This call to those who were listening, comes after some harsh words of judgement to people, who were not hearing the message of the kingdom that Jesus was declaring by word and deed. I take particular delight in the phrase; the 'unforced rhythms of grace'. That is how Jesus exercised his ministry; he dispensed grace. He always had the right words to say, avoiding the traps that were laid for him, being available to those who were in need, discipling the disciples and constantly being in the Father's presence. He modelled those rhythms of grace and it is something I find so attractive in him. In the busyness and constant demands, he managed to have that sense of a quiet centre rooted in the Father's love and company. I have struggled to experience this and I have found myself in a place where I have nothing left to give and at the stage of burnout, so these words speak tenderly and hopefully to me and, I am sure, to many others, in the cut and thrust of seeking to be a disciple.

My journey of faith following Jesus has left me with more unanswered questions. My faith is dependent upon relationship and not a list of concepts. This means that I am on a journey of discovery as the first disciples were and there is no knowing where that journey will lead me, but Jesus walks with me, and my fellow-disciples. Having witnessed many good and faithful disciples suffer, there are no guarantees for any of us. Being a disciple does not shelter us from the everyday struggles or from the very real problem of human suffering. In fact, it is important to recognise that in today's culture being a disciple of Jesus probably means that we are generally in a minority. I have found myself increasingly in awe of young people today, particularly at confirmation services, as they take promises to follow Jesus that will not be understood by many of their peers. When I was confirmed, nearly all of my friends were confirmed and I was part of a culture and context that meant, I was not alone. This is different now and it is much more difficult for people to stand up and confess faith in Jesus today. This is the world of today in which people are called to follow Jesus and it is more complex, where to believe anything is seen as odd. Add to that, a church that is increasingly reliant upon older members and there are difficult struggles for young people to make sense of their place within the life of the church. Following Jesus today means we have to rediscover that we are called to follow him to where people are and not just into the confines of church. "Being a disciple of Jesus is never about joining an exclusive sect, always about the desire to embrace the whole of humanity."[89] Our call to follow must lead us to the places where the broken, hurting and vulnerable are present so as we can bring Jesus to them by incarnating his presence in the mess. This is a challenging, demanding and yet exciting calling for all disciples.

One of the most difficult aspects of being a disciple is listening and being patient. I want to get things done and am very driven to accomplish that. So when I have to wait, it has been important to learn the frustration and yet the beauty of silence. "Silence is indispensable. It is a commonly overlooked element in language, but it must not be. Especially it must not be overlooked in prayer. It is not as if Jesus speaks the revelation of God in stories and metaphors, and now in prayer we get to say our piece. Silence, which in prayer consists mostly in attentive listening, is nonnegotiable."[90] There is something disturbing and beautiful about silence. Our present-day culture is full of noise and gadgets and it is hard to find anywhere where there is silence. I find it intriguing that when I go for a walk in the country or by the sea, so many people are listening to music on their earphones.

89   Perham, *Jesus and Peter*, 88.
90   Peterson, *Tell it Slant*, 160.

I find the silence that is interrupted by birdsong or the sounds of the sea speaks so deeply to my spirit. It is like the 'gentle whisper' that Elijah heard when God spoke to him when he was trying to run away from God. Waiting upon God is critical in our discipleship, as there are so many times we are confused and uncertain what to do or say. Listening to that still small voice is difficult but essential.

The command to go is easier for any activists; this is what we want to do. The difficulty is in discerning the task we believe we are called to do. If we are in a position of leadership, will those we seek to lead agree with us? Do we have to persuade, cajole or be patient? I have often found that leadership involves seeking to bring people with me, but there is a great tension in not knowing if I am being too cautious or if I need to be more courageous. These are difficult moments and I believe that it is at these times that the need for a team and those who share the vision is critical, as they can help in the journey of moving forward and inevitably facing change. However, there is also the time when the church needs to hear some prophetic voices calling us to recognise our failings and helping us seek God's help for the future. Discipleship will mean that we have to be willing to follow Jesus to where he goes and that is often to the most unexpected places with people we might not choose to be with. This is a demanding but exhilarating call. "We have succeeded in separating Christ from people, so that he is the icon of good and respectable people, and has little relevance to their own sordid and tangled lives. Jesus who lived and died as a 'friend of sinners' has been blasphemously translated into the enemy and judge of sinners."[91]

I want to finish this chapter with a word of encouragement, for all those, like me, who want to express their love for Jesus in being a disciple. Despite the fact that I recognise my brokenness and the enormity of the task, I find great encouragement in those first disciples. "From such a ragtag band Jesus founded a church that has not stopped growing."[92]

---

91   Riddell, *Threshold of the Future*, 123.
92   Yancey, *The Jesus I Never Knew*, 100.

CHAPTER *11*

NOT JUST ANY WEEK

Holy Week has always been an integral part of my journey with Jesus. In parish ministry, I was very involved in facilitating it and encouraging it. One of the joys in the parish of Ballyholme was this was something the local churches shared together. As a bishop, nearly every year I have spent Holy Week in different parishes around the diocese. However, my awareness of and involvement in Holy Week began as a child, when my local parish had special children's activities. Then, as a young leader, I helped with these special events. I find the title of the prayer book for Holy Week and Easter Day, compiled by my neighbour and friend, Bishop Harold, sums it up for me: *Week of all Weeks.*[93] For the purpose of this chapter, I want to reflect upon Jesus and some of the moments between Palm Sunday and Maundy Thursday.

I find it helpful to recognise, that there is a cloud hanging over the ministry of Jesus, that he keeps hinting at and which the disciples did not or did not want to grasp. "From quite an early stage of his ministry, Jesus evidently expected a violent death. The best evidence is not the very explicit predictions (which might be suspected of being written after the event), but the figurative or enigmatic references, those that pose a riddle of the kind Jesus was in the habit of posing when he talked about his identity or his mission: 'the bridegroom will be taken away', 'I have a baptism with which to be baptised', 'You will search for me, but you will not find me'... Jesus saw his death as the destiny the Father intended for him."[94] This shadow dominates this particular week. It is fascinating that the gospel accounts are particularly focused on this special and traumatic week in the life of Jesus.

93   Harold Miller, *Week of all Weeks*, (Belfast, Church of Ireland Press, 2015).
94   Bauckham, *Jesus: A Very Short Introduction*, (Oxford, Oxford University ress, 2011), 100-1. Reproduced with permission of the Licensor through PLSclear.

The entry into Jerusalem as recorded by Matthew enables creative liturgy for worship on Palm Sunday: the crowds cheering and singing, the involvement of children, the waving of palm branches and the image of Jesus on a donkey. This is an amazing scene at the beginning of this week. "It was for this extraordinary young teacher everyone was talking about, and was a most strange affair. Jesus mounted a dusty young donkey, which probably put him all of 20 centimetres above the crowds around him, and off he went, down the steep hill into the seething city. The disciples knew Jesus was making an important statement, though they weren't quite sure what it was."[95]

The week begins with this note of an expectant entry into Jerusalem, but the cloud of suffering is gathering and the rest of the week leaves us with many more questions. The disciples are about to experience a week that will cause much confusion and bewilderment. This procession into Jerusalem must have caused much interest, although the image of Jesus on a donkey, gently suggests all is not as it may appear. "In Jesus' triumphal entry, the daring crowd makes up the ragtag procession; the lame, the blind, the children, the peasants from Galilee and Bethany. Yes, there was a whiff of triumph on Palm Sunday, but not the kind of triumph that might impress Rome and not the kind that impressed crowds in Jerusalem for long either. What manner of king was this?"[96]

There were so many emotions in this particular event for all involved. The crowds were hopeful that they had found someone who would be their hero and rescue them from all that enslaved them. The disciples hoped that the one they had followed and given up everything for was eventually going to Jerusalem, for a showdown with those in authority, who had questioned him throughout his ministry. There were those who were observing, confused and concerned as to what this strange preacher and teacher was setting out to achieve. For Jesus, there was the obvious recognition that he was moving towards

---

95 Pritchard, *Living Jesus*, 66.
96 Yancey, *The Jesus I Never Knew*, 190.

the inevitability of a cruel death. This death was to express the amazing self-giving love of God by the trial, conviction and execution of an innocent man, the one who was the 'word made flesh'.

"The story of Jesus' grand, though surprising, entry into Jerusalem, then, is an object lesson in the mismatch between our expectations and God's answer. The bad news is that the crowds are going to be disappointed. But the good news is that their disappointment, though cruel, is at the surface level. Deep down, Jesus' arrival at the great city is indeed the moment when salvation is dawning."[97] This day of procession and cheering is to move quickly, as the passion narratives in the gospels spell out very clearly, from cheers of "Hosanna", to cries of "Crucify, Crucify". The voices of support are manipulated and distracted, and eventually lose confidence in the one they had been fascinated by for some time. There are others conspiring to find ways of getting rid of Jesus, the local political regime will show an unwillingness to make decisions and seek to find a way of washing their hands of this responsibility.

I have lived and worked within the church for decades and the religious world is intriguing. There are so many ways we can delude ourselves into thinking and believing that we are doing what God has called us to do. There are factions and various theological and liturgical preferences. The danger is always present, that we belong to one section of the church, and can see others as the enemy, or people we do not quite accept as being as 'right' as we are. There is the division in my own ecclesial home; between conservative and liberal, catholic and evangelical, charismatic and traditional. These divisions have many other variations and there is also the very significant one, in my own context, of Protestant and Roman Catholic. These are all painful divisions, among those of us, who are disciples of Jesus. "Most church people care deeply about what they are doing; otherwise they would not be doing it. This means they often have strong views about what ought to be done, and how things should be done. They derive emotional satisfaction from things being done in

---

97   Tom Wright, *Matthew for Everyone: Part 2,* (London, S.P.C.K., 2002), 69.

the way they prescribe. Not surprisingly, church issues more readily become matters of high principle than in most organisations."[98]

As a bishop, this has become so much more acute for me, as one of the most important promises at my ordination was: "Will you promote unity, peace, and love among all Christian people, and especially among those whom you serve?"[99] My answer appropriately was: "By the help of God, I will."[100] There are also many times when, as bishop, I am asked to find ways of dealing with conflict in parishes and this is particularly difficult, as there is the illusion that bishops have power to deal with such matters and indeed to fix them. I have discovered that bishops have authority in certain issues but no power, and perhaps that is not necessarily a bad thing! I find that much of these human divisions and tensions, are energy-sapping, and hinder the work of mission and extending God's kingdom. They can leave people frustrated and hurt, and when you add to that the religious dimension there is much complexity. As I reflect on that first Palm Sunday, I am very conscious of the different expectations that so many had, and how they were all so different, from what God was doing. They had misread the situation through their own perspective and not through the lens of God's amazing and unexpected grace.

It is one of the most difficult aspects of leadership in the church, being able to find ways of helping followers of Jesus to enable them to offer grace to one another. We are to be dispensers of grace, but sometimes we find it hardest to offer grace to fellow-pilgrims, as we cannot accept them as such. As part of our discipleship, we must rediscover what it is that matters on our journey. Like the crowds on Palm Sunday, we must see beyond the human story, and remember the amazing divine story of God, doing something that we cannot fully understand, and that ultimately judgement is his, based on an eternal and beautiful love that knows no bounds.

---

98   Fraser Watts, Rebecca Sage and Sue Savage, *Psychology for Ministry*, (Abingdon: Routledge, 2002), 255.
99   *The Book of Common Prayer*, (Dublin, Columba Press, 2004), 578.
100 Ibid., 578.

As this week unfolds, there are encounters and incidents that will become part of the story for millions of people who have followed Jesus ever since. The Last Supper and the washing of the disciples' feet are still part of the story we tell in our churches every Holy Week. These are disciples whose lives will never be the same again as they live with the memories of this incredible week in the life of Jesus. They were participants but also observers, as events were way beyond their control and initially their understanding.

"Until that moment the whole point of things had been for someone to get on top, and once he had gotten on top to stay on top or else attempt to get farther up. But here this man already on top - who was rabbi, teacher, master - suddenly got down on the bottom and began to wash the feet of his followers. In that one act Jesus overturned the whole social order. Hardly comprehending what was happening, even his disciples were almost horrified by his behaviour."[101] A profound and intimate moment for the disciples as Jesus washed their feet. There are some churches that still enact this beautiful symbol as part of the liturgy of Maundy Thursday. I have taken part in it and it is disturbing and humbling. I only discovered this liturgical practice of feet washing later in my ministry and it is such an important reminder of the upside down world of God's kingdom. Jesus washed the disciples' feet, to remind them and us, that his ministry is one of service not power. In our calling, as individual disciples, and as Christian communities, we must model this ministry of service and self-giving especially, in the mess on our doorsteps. The kingdom of God as seen in the ministry of Jesus is one of service and humility. "Following that example has not gotten any easier in two thousand years."[102]

I have always enjoyed the moments of family celebrations when we spend time around a table hearing each other's stories and enjoying being together. The dynamic has certainly changed since becoming a grandfather; I am the senior member of this family and the perspective changes. It makes me think much more of those who shaped me and

---

101 M. Scott Peck, *The Different Drum*, (New York, Touchstone, 1988), 293.
102 Yancey, *The Jesus I Never Knew*, 192.

how grateful I am for them. It also makes me think of the future, wondering what will happen to those I love and cherish. There are no morbid thoughts in this, but a genuine sense of wonder and hope. There are also many other times when meals are moments of friendship and blessing: a gathering of friends, a celebration among work colleagues or an anniversary dinner for two. "The sharing of food and the hearing of each other's stories is the making of community."[103]

Throughout scripture, meals and celebrations are important markers and reminders of the journey of faith for individuals and the community of faith. "The great Jewish festivals all function in this way, most of them connected to the retelling of some part of the story of how God has rescued Israel from slavery in Egypt. Supreme among the festivals was Passover, when they not only told the story of how God had liberated them, but used to recline on couches at the table; in that world, free people didn't just sit, they reclined."[104] The context for the Last Supper was set, and the disciples were sent to prepare the room for this deeply significant meal and encounter. It is difficult not to see this scene through the eyes of having received the Eucharist for nearly 50 years. It is very difficult to see it afresh and as the disciples did. I also do not have a Jewish background to understand in full the nuances and to have the emotional and spiritual understanding of previous Passover meals. However, this is a highly-charged moment, as Jesus is preparing his disciples for his death. He has spoken about his death, but it appears as if they understandably have not realised the enormity of what was about to happen.

This moment in the journey for the disciples has become something that countless Christians have done ever since, and, tragically, it has also become a source of division among those of us who are his followers. "It is nothing less than astonishing, considering the conflicts and variations within church practice that mark the Christian church across the continents and centuries, that this Supper has been eaten so consistently and similarly under Jesus' command 'do this'.

103 Adams, *Cave Refectory Road,* 30.
104 Wright, *Mark for Everyone,* 193.

We have come up with different theologies for understanding what Jesus is doing as he feeds us in this Meal and what we are doing when we receive it, but we sit at Table (or kneel or stand) with Jesus as host we do and continue to do exactly as he commanded us: we eat the bread and drink the cup in 'remembrance of me' and 'proclaim the Lord's death until he comes'. "[105]

It is difficult to describe the amazing joy and delight it is to celebrate the Eucharist in various parishes across the diocese. I also had the joy and privilege of being a parish priest, and standing at the same table every week, with a community, of which you are a part, which was incredibly special. These are holy moments that are part of the delight of being a priest. In these celebrations, we are doing so "in remembrance of me". This is a mystery beyond words, and a moment of encounter for the individual, and the community, as Jesus is present with us in the mess of our lives. "'Remembrance of me'. The Greek term, *anamnesis*, translated 'remembrance', is more than a mental activity; it is a reenacting in the Supper itself, what Jesus did. It involves more than just refreshing the memory of what Jesus did; it involves us in participating right now, around this Table, in what he did and continues to do."[106]

We are also proclaiming again that Jesus died for the sins of the world. The Eucharist is a dramatic presentation of the gospel or an enacted parable that seeks to point to the mystery of Jesus and his death as the lamb of God who takes away the sin of the world.

It is such a wonderful parable of how Jesus comes to us in our brokenness. He offers us his broken body, to bring us his amazing grace and mercy in tangible gifts, the bread and wine, which become to us his body and blood. Jesus takes the ordinary gifts of bread and wine and makes them special for us. He also takes our ordinariness and uses us to bring him to others. This jewel, that is, Jesus, transforms

105 Eugene Peterson, *Christ Plays in Ten Thousand Places*, (Michigan, Eerdmans, 2005), 200.
106 Gregory Dix, *The Shape of the Liturgy*, Revised Edition, (London: Bloomsbury, 2015), 161.

us by grace as he takes our humanity and vulnerability and makes us channels of that same amazing grace.

One of the most important aspects of our Eucharistic liturgy in the Church of Ireland is the 'Great Silence', which comes after everyone has received the Eucharist. I believe this is so appropriate and necessary, and should be for more than a few seconds, and everyone should observe it. As we receive these holy mysteries, it is right that we pause and hold our breath and recognise the amazing gift that we have received that is beyond words or definition!

> "Let all mortal flesh keep silence
> and with fear and trembling stand;
> ponder nothing earthly minded,
> for with blessing in his hand
> Christ our God descendeth,
> our full homage to demand.
>
> King of kings, yet born of Mary,
> as of old on earth he stood,
> Lord of lords, in human vesture -
> in the body and the blood -
> he will give to all the faithful
> his own self for heavenly food."[107]

---

107 Hymn 427 'Let All Mortal Flesh Keep Silence' verses 1 and 2, *Irish Church Hymnal,* (Dublin, Columba Press, 2003).

CHAPTER 12

IT IS FINISHED

They were some of the most difficult and painful moments in parish ministry. Raw grief is excruciating. The pain of loss, and the loss of a loved one, is a life-changing moment, as life will never be the same again. There are scenes that will stay with me forever. A parent telling me not to say that her death is alright because his daughter is in Heaven. His pain is something he will have to try and live with forever. Another parent who had to find ways of telling his family that one of their children had taken his own life. Two young parents discovering their child had died in her cot during the night. Words and trite religious cliches so often insult the pain of those who have been bereaved. Death is deeply disturbing and the web of grief leaves so many unresolved questions and the cruel finality of parting. Daily we see pictures and scenes of devastation and loss, as people across the world lose loved ones in profoundly tragic events. These moments tear at the very fabric of body, mind and soul, leaving shock, numbness and grief. In the middle of the human struggle with grief, we also know that death is certain for all of us. It is an indisputable fact that we will die. There is uncertainty, as to when and how, but it will happen.

In my journey with Jesus, I have found him so often in the mess and pain of people's lives. It should be no surprise that the ending of the gospel narratives bring us to the mess and bewilderment of his death. This is no ordinary death and the scriptures seek to point us to hidden depths of this dramatic conclusion to his earthly life. The gospel writers give us accounts of Jesus' death and there are different nuances and styles.

In this chapter I want to reflect upon this death, and do so as if I were leading a three-hour Good Friday devotional service, something

I have done for many years. I am using the structure as outlined in 'A Good Friday Three Hours Service The Seven Words From The Cross'.[108] Reflecting upon these holy moments, as Jesus nears his death, I am very conscious that we are trying to comprehend a mystery. Hence, I want to meditate rather than study or seek to dissect something that I will never fully comprehend. "Nothing in Jesus's life is more meticulously documented than his dying and death. 'Dead and Buried', as our Apostles' Creed has it, a death every bit as physical as ours will be. A divine event was enacted in the death of Jesus. His death, a willed and sacrificial death, was an offering for the death-dealing sins of the world, a death that conquered death. This is a great mystery, perhaps the greatest mystery in the cosmos, in heaven and earth, and, strictly speaking unfathomable."[109]

"Father forgive them for they know not what they are doing."[110] This phrase clashes so profoundly with anger, rage, violence and conflict that haunts so many parts of the world. In my own context, there is still the real pain of those who were victims and are survivors of the violence that tore apart communities in Northern Ireland and still enslaves us in our troubled and painful past. In the mess of our situation, we need to find ways of sensitively and carefully bringing healing and restoration. The words of forgiveness have rung out throughout the pain, but they are so difficult. There are issues raised by these disturbing questions and there are no easy answers, but the worst we can do is to ignore the real and deep pain in the hope that it will somehow disappear.

I have also visited South Sudan and heard horrendous stories of conflict and the violence that human beings have done to each other. The people that I met were numb with the pain of civil war and haunted by their memories. This pain is real and is continuing, as

108 Miller, *Week of all Weeks*, 51.
109 Eugene Peterson, *As Kingfisher's Catch Fire*, (London, Hodder and Stoughton 2017), 257.
110 NRSV Luke 23:34.

there is as yet no end to the internal conflict that has so damaged this young fledgling country. If you are interested, please pray for South Sudan, that sometime soon peace will take root again.

Through my role as a member of the World Council of Churches Central Committee, I have met people from other parts of the globe caught up in war and conflict, not least the Middle East. There are so many tragic accounts, of what deep-seated wounds can cause people to do to one another. Yet in the midst of the conflict, there are also amazing stories of peace-making and reconciliation.

The words of forgiveness as recorded by Luke are in stark contrast to the many words of anger and hate that are at work in conflict and violence. "For me, the utter powerlessness of God is that God forgives. I hold myself in a position of power by not forgiving myself or others. God does not hold on to that position of power. God forgives the world for being broken and poor. God forgives us for not being all that we thought we had to be and even for what God wanted us to be. This is probably why we fall in love with such a God."[111] Jesus, even in his death, recognised the chaos and mess of the world and speaks words of hope and new beginnings.

"Today you will be with me in paradise"[112]

This is a very human scene, as there are two criminals being crucified, hanging either side of Jesus. One of the criminals taunts and teases Jesus, as do the soldiers; perhaps he thought this might help him. The other recognises the innocence of Jesus, and shows deep discernment of what was happening at this moment.

In this passage there are other messages that resonate with the two thieves and their attitude to Jesus. "Jesus combines the clear statement of his own intention, to suffer Israel's fate on her behalf, with the clear warning, echoing the warnings throughout the gospel, for those who do not follow him. Luke makes the same point in a different way by contrasting the two who were crucified on either

111 Rohr, *Everything Belongs,* 153.
112 NRSV Luke 23:43.

side of Jesus. The one taunts, but the other expresses Luke's view of the whole scene. Jesus once again, is dying the death appropriate for the rebel, the brigand, the criminal; he is bearing the sins of many, innocent though he himself is."[113]

It is fascinating how various people react to Jesus differently. However, I want to recognise that one of the great sadnesses of my experience with people is that many have rejected the beauty of Jesus because of those who claim to follow him. I want to recognise how, as disciples, all of us have failed to present the wonder of this amazing grace that the thief witnessed as he watched Jesus die. In the mess of our own lives, I want to remember that the most important gift I bring to this life and journey with Jesus, is my brokenness.

"Here is your son...here is your mother"[114]

In the midst of the enormity of what was happening and facing his own death, these few verses come as an interlude. They are a reminder of where this life on earth began, and the amazing young girl that gave birth to Jesus in the mess of Bethlehem. The humanity expressed is critical; it is the critical connection Jesus has with us. His concern is for his mother who, at this point, must have been remembering all the things he had said and yet again pondering them in her heart. To watch her child die was horrific enough without the very public and humiliating death he endured. Where were the promises of God and how he was a very special child? The pain in her heart is beyond comprehension and yet she stays to be as close to him, as any mother would.

My admiration for Mary is immense. She is such an example of a parent's love and of a parent's refusal to give up on her child. The courage and resolve she showed is, in some sense, rewarded by Jesus by recognising her pain and offering her some consolation in the love of one of his friends and disciples to care for her. This is such a tender and emotional moment that acknowledges Mary for her wonderful, selfless, care to a very special son.

---

113 Wright, *Luke for Everyone*, 284.
114 NRSV John 19:26-7.

"My God, my God, why have you forsaken me?"[115]

In this cry, we meet a mystery beyond comprehension. The emptiness and the finality of death, nothingness, void and the end. Jesus does not escape the inescapable bewilderment of death and the final human moment. This is a cry from Jesus, which highlights the enormity of his death, and of the lamb of God taking away the sins of the world. Somehow the Godhead is involved in this cry when, for this moment of eternity, there is fracture and pain, that is abandonment and emptiness. "And welling up from his lifetime of biblically based prayer there came, as though by a reflex, a cry not of rebellion, but of despair and sorrow, yet still a despair that, having lost contact with God, still asks God why this should be. The question of Job - why do the innocent suffer? - mingles with the question not only of the Psalmists but of millions in the ancient and modern world, and becomes the question, to use later Christian language, that God himself uses when forsaken by god, that God the Son uses when forsaken, unthinkable by God the Father. Unless we wrestle with this question we not only cut ourselves off from understanding the central Christian mystery and glory: we trivialise the gospel which meets the world at its point of deepest need."[116]

I have always found it hard to fathom the depths of this moment, when all that causes pain and hurt is borne by Jesus, and the abandonment causes him to cry as he does. There are different models used to try and describe what is happening, although somehow none of them, of themselves, can capture the enormity and mystery of Jesus at this moment being in the chaos and mess of the pain and hurt of the created order. "Then we come up against the paradoxical and uncontainable action of God that breaks all our images and models apart. God wins a victory through being defeated; God the almighty meekly offers himself as a ransom; God the creator of all things lives as a human being to show human beings the truth about themselves; God the judge offers himself for judgement; God to whom all

115 NRSV Mark 15:34.
116 Wright, *Mark for Everyone*, 217.

sacrifices are offered lays himself upon the altar for us to dismember. God goes where our imagination cannot reach because our love is too timid and our words inadequate. Jesus has to die because our 'model' of God is tame and can never reach the depths of our need."[117]

"I am thirsty."[118]

This is a very brief prayer that recognises the human pain of dying. Of the seven sayings or prayers from the cross, this is the only one in which Jesus is facing the physical struggle of dying. There is no escaping the physical pain and anguish of this death and of this particularly cruel death. "There is pain: the body shutting down, lungs failing, heart failing, kidneys failing. In Jesus' death this leave-taking of his body was experienced as excruciating thirst: 'I thirst'."[119]

In penning these reflections, I am conscious of how there can be a tendency to focus on the divinity of Jesus, and in the process, we lose sight of the sheer sadness and desolation of this very human moment in the life of Jesus: the abandonment already mentioned in his cry of despair, the taunts of those soldiers who were watching, the sadness of seeing his mother and the physical struggle of trying to survive with the pain. The disciples were frightened and of little use at this stage and in fact the end was very near. These are important moments for us to remember when we seek to walk with others in their pain; Jesus understands the horror of death, abandonment and dying.

"It is finished"[120]

It is a joy to recognise the various ways that each of the gospels brings us different ways of telling us about Jesus and his life, essentially the same story from different perspectives. "St John (and who dares summarise his portrait in a sentence or two?) shows us that the Word who is made flesh in Jesus is also at work in all of creation; that life

---

117 Jane Williams, *Why Did Jesus Have To Die*, (London, SPCK, 2016), 24.
118 NRSV John 19:28
119 Peterson, *Tell it Slant*, 256.
120 NRSV John 19:30

and judgement are present in the here and now, and that the Passion in itself is victory and glory."[121]

It is hard to imagine that this is a cry of victory rather than of defeat. Once Jesus began the journey towards Jerusalem on Palm Sunday, there was inevitability about the outcome; he had said many times that this would be the end result of his ministry. To those who journeyed with him, this certainly was not what they expected and they did not see this as victory at this moment. "'It's finished!', 'It's all done!' 'It's complete!' He has finished the work that the father had given him to do (17.4). He has loved 'to the very end' his own who were in the world (13.1). He has accomplished the full and final task. The words that I've translated 'It's all done!' Is actually a single word in the original language. It's the word that people would write on a bill after it had been paid. The bill is dealt with. It's finished. The price has been paid. Yes, says John: and Jesus' work is now complete, in that sense as in every other. It is upon this finished, complete work that his people from that day to this can stake their lives."[122]

This is indeed a profound and holy moment, when God's amazing grace is expressed in the most profound way, as the lamb of God takes away the sins of the world.

"Father, into your hands I commend my spirit"[123]

This is the moment when Jesus dies. We pause ... we remember ... and we give thanks for God's amazing love. A love that pursues us and never gives up on us. These are moments that are critical on our journey with Jesus. It is so important to remember why we are followers of Jesus. It is not fear that motivates us, or a compulsion that is driven by us feeling we ought to. This discipleship is rooted in being captured, by this love that knows no bounds, expressed in this piece of wood, in the form of a cross. It is recognising Jesus and his

121 Michael Ramsey, *Through The Year With Michael Ramsey*, ed. Margaret Duggan (London, SPCK, Re-issued 2009), 67.
122 Wright, *John for Everyone*, 131.
123 NRSV Luke 23:46

dependence upon the Father, even when he felt abandoned. It is being able to live in the present moment, recognising that God is with us no matter what the circumstances. We are always with him and our childlike faith can help us rest in him.

PERSONAL REFLECTION

It never ceases to amaze me that, every time I reflect upon the events of the first Good Friday, my heart is warmed and my spirit is renewed, as I am in awe of the amazing grace made known to us all in Jesus. There are so many people who were part of this day whom we haven't mentioned. There is Judas who wanted Jesus to bring a different end to this journey, and he realised the mistake he made and paid a great price. There is Pontius Pilate, who tried to wash his hands of this miscarriage of justice, and his wife who was deeply disturbed by her dreams. There are the religious leaders of his day, who could not grasp what Jesus was trying to do, and I am not sure we would have, had we been watching the events from their perspective. There are the disciples, who must have been fearful for their own lives. There are also the women, other than his mother, who stood by the cross, watching helplessly and weeping. However, I want to connect this day back to Bethlehem, and Jesus coming into the mess of the world. "'The word became flesh and lived among us.' God didn't just create us, didn't just love from afar, didn't just work in history to rescue us and strengthen us and heal us. God's true nature appears in the real, substantial, material, physical reality of Jesus among us, Jesus just like us, Jesus beside us. And beside us not just in joy and celebration, but beside us in horror, in agony, in isolation and abandonment."[124]

This surely has to be our motivation, in how we seek to be Jesus, alongside others, who are so often forgotten, ignored, or those who feel abandoned.

---

124 Samuel Wells, *Hanging by a Thread*, (Norwich, Canterbury Press, 2016), 60.

Cross Tree

A tree is something
You have to
Get to the
Top of.
Jesus climbed his,
With some
Assistance,
And stayed there,
Fixed by love,
To set us free
From the
Mad rush
To dominate
Our fellows.
'Take up your
Cross,'
He said, 'and
Follow me.'[125]

125 Ann Lewin, 'Cross Tree', *Watching for the Kingfisher*, (Norwich, Canterbury Press, 2004), 21.

CHAPTER 13

WHAT?

I have always found it very difficult to preach on Easter Day! A strange admission for someone who has been in ordained ministry for over 37 years, and 11 of those as a bishop. Yet I am convinced that the disciples found that first Easter Day bewildering and confusing. They were still reeling from grief and disappointment from the death of Jesus. "No one ever told me grief felt so like fear. I am not afraid, but the sensation is being like afraid. The same fluttering in my stomach, the same restlessness, the yawning. I keep on swallowing ... There is a sort of invisible blanket between the world and me. I find it hard to take in what anyone says. Or perhaps, hard to want to take it in."[126] There was a sliver of light opening up as the women were announcing that Jesus was not in the tomb. The light and hope of Easter Day took some time to sink in, for the disciples to be certain of what they based the rest of their lives on. When preaching on Easter Day, I always find myself still wanting to wrestle with the confusion of grief that will ease and become a new-found joy, but it just feels too soon on Easter morning. I find a soulmate in Thomas, who needed to see Jesus, and place his hands in the wounds before he would believe. The news of resurrection was a bewildering step of faith and this surely took time to assimilate. In my thinking, there would surely have been difficulty in moving from fear, guilt, and grief to such unimaginable joy. "Right up to the last minute we dared hope that God would send in some angels, stop the whole charade and let everyone see how wrong they were and how right Jesus was. But no last minute rescue came. Only death came. Bloody, sweaty, filthy, ugly death. Just before

---

126 C.S. Lewis, *A Grief Observed*, (London, Faber and Faber, 1961), 7.

he died, it seemed that even he had lost faith. 'My God, my God, why have you forsaken me? he cried. Now. Now he is dead. The adventure of Jesus is dead and done."[127]

These disciples were terrified and it was going to take some convincing for them to find hope again. The various gospel writers give us different accounts of that first Easter morning and the news of resurrection. There is uncertainty about the ending of Mark's account and the general consensus among scholars is that the alternative two endings are not written by Mark. That leaves us with Mark finishing before recounting the resurrection. "But I think it far more likely that he wrote a conclusion ... The ending may not have been very long but it will have been important as the intended conclusion to the book, drawing the themes to their proper destination."[128]

Matthew, Luke and John give us the details of various resurrection accounts and encounters that help us gain awareness and insight into how these fearful and confused disciples were to set out on a journey that would begin a journey of faith, which we have entered into today. These three accounts begin with the role of women, and that in itself is amazing, Mary Magdalene in particular. "If someone in the 1st Century had wanted to invent a story about people seeing Jesus, they wouldn't have dreamed of giving the star part to a woman, let alone Mary Magdalene."[129] It should not surprise us that yet again the unexpected is part of the Easter moment. The upside down world of God's kingdom is present again in the life-changing moment of resurrection. "As almost every scholar notes, in that society women were not trusted to give evidence. They were thought to be more emotional than men, and especially in religious matters apt to be credulous, too easily swayed by emotion. Celsus, a 2nd Century intellectual despised of Christianity, dismissed the alleged testimony of Mary Magdalene by calling her 'a hysterical female'. Luke's gospel candidly admits that at

127 McLaren, *We Make the Road by Walking*, 201-2.
128 Wright, *Mark for Everyone*, 223-4.
129 Wright, *John for Everyone*, 147.

first the male disciples did not believe these women's reports."[130] God takes the ordinary and makes them special. I also find it intriguing that Jesus, throughout the narratives of his life, gives such prominence to women, as this was counter cultural. The church, at times, is still struggling with this important lesson of the gospels.

I want to reflect on some of these encounters that intrigue me and have helped me on my journey with Jesus. The differences in the accounts do not disturb me. However, the incredible event of resurrection, as I have read the biblical revelation, is the only explanation as to why this strange group of Jesus' followers gave up everything for someone who changed their lives forever, and this was surely rooted in resurrection rather than make believe.

There are obvious differences in the various narratives presented in each of the gospels. As someone who studied history and is used to pursuing historical fact, these variations might concern me, although having studied Irish history, it is interesting how there are differences, depending on the cultural and political backgrounds of those giving the historical accounts. I once appeared in court as a witness to a road traffic accident and it was fascinating how different people gave a different account of the same accident, as they emphasised different facets of the same incident, as seen from their perspective. In the context of the gospels there is also the need to convey the meaning of these events. It is important to understand and appreciate the culture and context of the gospel writers. "These differences might disturb people who don't understand that storytelling in the ancient world was driven less by a duty to convey the true details accurately and more by a desire to proclaim a true meaning powerfully."[131]

There is one of the resurrection accounts, in particular, that has enriched my reflection, and indeed I find this encounter a constant help for reading and contemplation. It is Luke's account of the journey by some disciples on the road to Emmaus. The disciples on this journey reveal the devastation they were experiencing, as

130 Bauckham, *Jesus: A Very Short Introduction*, 105.
131 McLaren, *We Make the Road by Walking*, 210.

they sought to make sense of what had happened to Jesus on the previous Friday. They were experiencing the reality of Psalm 42 and Psalm 43: "Why are you so downcast, O my soul?" They were encountering the raw emotions of grief, anger, guilt, denial and fear. Jesus dying did not make sense, and their world was one of devastation and loss. In their walking as friends, with the stranger who accompanied them, they were beginning to verbalise their hurt and trying to grapple with the confusion.

There are particular elements in the Emmaus record that I find illuminating; friendship, scripture and Eucharist. I have already discussed the importance of fellow-disciples as we journey and I believe it is critical to our well-being as disciples. I grew up in a religious culture that emphasised personal discipleship and relationship with Jesus, to the detriment of our sense of corporate identity and relationship to and with our fellow-disciples. There was a limited recognition of 'Church' as the 'Body of Christ', and its fundamental importance to all who follow Jesus. It is about accountability and us all belonging to Jesus together. This is particularly important if we are to be able to incarnate the presence of Jesus in local communities, as we do this together as fellow-disciples in a community of faith. "Since God is none other than the divine trinitarian persons in relationship, a relationship characterised by a mutuality that can only be characterised by love, the 'imago Dei' is ultimately human persons in loving relationship as well. Only in relationship, as persons in community, are we able to reflect the fullness of divine character."[132]

These disciples, as they journeyed with grief, found enormous strength and comfort wrestling with their pain together. This is my experience on my journey with Jesus; I have found such wisdom, strength and challenge as I have journeyed with fellow-disciples. We must not ignore the call to make disciples, and to ensure that we are nurturing our own discipleship. I also reflect upon my experience of practicing faith in a community that has heard much about Jesus. It

132 John R. Franke, *The Character of Theology*, (Michigan, Baker Academic, 2005), 181.

has also grown tired of religious jargon. The faith that was presented to me growing up was about the afterlife, and not about making life better on earth for the many who struggle to make sense of conflict, religion and suffering. The incarnation becomes the theological key to discover our calling to be the presence of Jesus in the mess and not to stand in judgement. The danger as I see it has been that the religious community offered life jackets for eternity rather than helping people to swim in the mess.

The value of scripture is something that I learnt from a young age. Part of my upbringing was to learn scripture off by heart. I apparently was good at it; I have a photographic memory, which was useful for remembering material for history exams. In the religious world, scripture can also be used to justify our position and to find ways of condemning others. It is a powerful tool, but it can be misused. The liturgical framework, in which I have worshipped all my life as a disciple has helped me see the way in which scripture can shape our praying and our worship. I find in scripture new discoveries and constant challenges and sometimes I am confused and questioning, like Job. However, it is something I cherish because it points to Jesus as the 'word made flesh'. "As scripture, the Bible is therefore 'authoritative' for the community that regards it as scripture, and then that community is shaped by these divine encounters, which continue to spark new encounters with the divine."[133]

The disciples, as they journeyed, had the recent events explained through the lens of scripture and they had the best possible teacher to help them. The revelation of God that we have in the pages of scripture is such a special gift and we need to continue to wrestle with, and be formed by, scripture, as it continues to reveal to us the living word, the Jesus who journeyed with the disciples on the road to Emmaus.

The beautiful moment, when they recognised the stranger who travelled with them, comes in the breaking of bread, a Eucharistic moment. This moment must have resonated with the disciples so

---

133 Robin B. Meyers, *Saving Jesus from the Church*, (San Francisco, Harper-One, 2009), 29-30.

soon after the Last Supper of the Thursday the week before. The emotion of the final meal, the washing of the disciples' feet, the last moments before Jesus was arrested; then, after they had the scriptures explained, they recognised him as he broke the bread and gave thanks. This sacrament is something that has divided the Christian churches, and arguments over the mystery of this God-given gift are very sad. It is impossible to define something that is a mystery of God's grace. I have come to cherish the Eucharist, and I use this title deliberately, as it means thanksgiving or gratitude. I am very grateful for this sacrament, which is a constant reminder of Jesus and his death, but also his resurrection, as he is with us always.

The wonderful way that Luke in his account keeps the delight of scripture and Eucharist together is something that I find particularly important, but maybe that is because I am an Anglican who views word and sacrament as inseparable. The word roots us in our salvation story recorded in scripture and the sacrament is a parable that helps us meditate on the wonder and awe of Jesus present with us always.

The joy of this account of the journey to Emmaus is that as they walked Jesus was with them. He was always present, even when they were deep in grief and confusion. Jesus was present with them, even when they did not recognise him. This has been so important on my journey. On those difficult and dark days, which there are bound to be because we are human, Jesus is always with us. He is with us in the confusion and pain of our lives. He also wants to help us to help others to discover this, by our living out his presence in our local communities, and we do this by doing it together as fellow-disciples.

I mentioned earlier that I had a kindred spirit in Thomas. He has become known as 'doubting Thomas'. This is somewhat unfair, as Matthew does mention that there were some other disciples, who were struggling to believe. Thomas is important to the accounts because there are many who, like him, find it hard to believe. He had at times found it difficult to understand what Jesus was teaching; "Thomas said to him, 'Lord, we do not know the way you are going.

How can we know the way?'"[134] He had missed the gathering of disciples on Easter Day when Jesus had appeared to the others. Now he wanted to check for himself that this was Jesus. There is a word of encouragement to those who will not see Jesus and yet believe. This is true for millions of disciples who have believed without seeing and we are numbered with them.

There are still many today who find faith difficult. Those who have had a bad experience of church. Some who will find the church building a strange world where they do not feel they belong. Others who imagine that what we do on Sundays is odd and they would not know how to join in with our strange practices and customs. Many believe that we are judgemental and have no fun. Our responsibility is to show them the loveliness of this risen Jesus, who helped Thomas believe. In today's culture, it will be important that we do this by building trust and friendship and by how we live and act. We only use words when we are asked to and give account of why we love Jesus. I do envy the disciples, because they saw Jesus, and witnessed firsthand the great miracle of resurrection.

I cannot leave reflecting upon the resurrection without mentioning Peter. I have always loved Peter, the straightforward, foot-in-the-mouth, vulnerable and failed disciple. He messed up and he knew it. His denial is particularly difficult because he had been warned by Jesus that he would, and he had sworn that he would never deny Jesus. "Peter had failed in the most devastating way possible. This was not just misplaced enthusiasm or misunderstanding; it was deliberate, emphatic, blasphemous failure."[135]

The restoration of Peter is a key element of the account John gives us. The three-times questioning of Peter and his love for Jesus, mirror his three clear denials. It is obvious from the account that Peter finds this encounter very painful, as it is a reminder of his failure and also a questioning of his love. Yet this encounter became life-changing as it inspired, renewed and forgave. I find in Peter such inspiration

134 NRSV John 14:5
135 , Tomlin, *Looking Through the Cross*, 153.

because we see his brokenness, his humanity, and his deep love for Jesus. He was so devastated by his denial because he loved Jesus. His love is real and yet fragile, because of his humanness. He gets it wrong, but he does not fail to get up and try again. The amazing grace of Jesus restores, heals and forgives. That is something that gives me encouragement and hope. "Peter is follower, disciple, evangelist, witness, friend; and as such he is an example and encourager. We are drawn to him, inspired by him, because in him so much remained for a long time imperfect and unresolved."[136]

What a few days for those who loved Jesus. The rollercoaster ride that turned their lives upside down. They had experienced so much already on their journey with him, since his baptism, and his call for them to follow him. What a story they had to tell, and the gospel writers have given such glimpses of this extraordinary man called Jesus. Their accounts point us to that most amazing miracle that he was indeed 'the word made flesh', God in human form. This is a mystery, but the resurrection is what declared this to be true. That is why the disciples started on the journey to spread the good news, they had seen the risen Jesus, a journey which we are part of today.

The first Easter was an amazing moment, when Jesus, the jewel in the mess, gave all his disciples, then and now, the potential to continue his ministry as a 'friend of sinners'. We are called to declare his continued presence in the world by how we live out this resurrection. I will reflect on some situations where I have found fellow-disciples, seeking to do this in very ordinary ways. We are invited by God to continue to tell the story of his unconditional love made known in Jesus.

> "What ending does the story come to now?
> Might we feel God's hand upon us,
> God's breath upon our faces,
> God's kiss?
> Might we find hope beyond all imagining.
> and grief turned all to joy,

---

136 Perham, *Jesus and Peter*, 110.

new birth,
new life beyond all expectation?
Might we tumble to it all,
and know that we have stumbled upon
resurrection?

I cannot answer that.
But I can assure you
that God tried to teach Abraham and Sarah
to prepare for surprises."[137]

137 Trevor Dennis, 'The Walk to Emmaus', *The Three Faces of Christ*, (London, SPCK, 2009), 57-58. Reproduced with permission of the Licensor through PLSclear.

CHAPTER 14

FINDING JESUS TODAY

As a bishop, I have found myself increasingly struggling with the disconnect between church and local community. Most of our energy as local parishes is in helping those who belong to church. The resources and capacity for anything else are very difficult. There is also the growing realisation that the good news we proclaim is not just for humanity, but for the whole of creation. Planet earth is in serious trouble and we are slowly destroying the created order we believe was given to us to care for by God. In my early experience in discipleship, and indeed in ordained ministry, the overwhelming issue for the faith communities I was part of was personal salvation and the afterlife. "Of course, there are those who still see the Church as a holy lifeboat, attempting to save as many as possible from the sinking vessel that is modern culture, and that any attempt to adapt to it will result in us getting pulled down too, but it seems impossible to defend this position when we read of a God who got stuck in and involved in a culture at every conceivable level."[138]

As part of my sabbatical, in which I was seeking to focus on Jesus, I also visited some places where there is a genuine attempt to connect faith and local community. They are similar and yet different, but they are all part of what Church Army UK and Ireland is seeking to do in incarnating the presence of Jesus in places where the local church would not have the resources and ability to do so. "The nature of institutional thinking is monopolistic and unitary: it thinks it is the only show on the road and the only way things can be done. Therefore, I have noticed that, in this way of seeing, any new people wanting to join the Church as institution do so by being incorporated into

138 Kester Brewin, *The Complex Christ*, (London, SPCK, 2004), 79.

exactly its style, under its rule."[139] There are some difficult tensions in seeking to facilitate a change in perceptions and thinking within the structures of church. Many of the questions we ask are rooted in our own background and history. We want to know how we can get more young people and families into church. We want to know what things we can do that will attract people to church. We want to know how we can ensure that our buildings are not damaged and yet open them up for wider use. We want to know where the money to do new things will come from. We want to find ways of looking to the future but at the same time will resist change and innovation that disturbs. These are important and vital issues and concerns in local parishes that are struggling to keep going, but increasingly I believe they are the wrong questions! There is a danger that the questions are about maintaining what we have and standing still or declining, rather than imagining a new future.

Reflecting upon the life of Jesus, I have been reminded, encouraged and disturbed as I discover afresh how he spent so much time in the chaos and mess of the world bringing blessing and challenge. He was always spending time with those who didn't belong, or who were on the edge, or who were judged as not good enough. How do we in today's culture and church find ways of modelling the ministry of Jesus as the church called to mission? There are no easy answers or slick programmes to follow; Jesus met with people in their mess and by being there made a difference. He did not fix the mess, but somehow by his presence helped people in the mess find a new way of seeing themselves and living in their context. He helped people discover that they were indeed made in the image of God. I have also observed and spoken with my adult children and their friends who find church a strange place. These are people who have faith, but find traditional church does not connect with their lives and experiences. "Churches, for the most part, have failed to address the nagging anxieties and deep seated fears of the people, focused instead upon

139 George Lings, *Reproducing Churches*, (Oxford, BRF, 2017), 21.

outdated or secondary issues and proposing tired or trite solutions."[140] They particularly want to engage with social and justice issues that are all around us in our society. The role of small groups and the ability to discuss, probe and work out their faith in context are critical. Faith in today's culture appears to be more about questions than answers. There is the need to wrestle with scripture and culture to enable a faith that can be lived out in daily life, which does not answer questions people are not asking. We must give space for people to ask their own questions and the potential to wrestle with these together in the context of their daily lives through the lens of scripture and the inspiration of the Holy Spirit.

In my role of oversight, I find that much of my energy is taken up in fire fighting, dealing with internal conflicts that I cannot resolve or trying to find ways of maintaining the parish structures that I believe are increasingly not fit for purpose. In the middle of this struggle, there are so many faithful clergy and people who are giving of their time, talents and energy. These are amazing people, who have borne the heat and burden of the day, and I cannot commend them enough, but I long to find ways of helping them do things differently. "All around the world Christians are bursting out of the local church, not to replace it but to start alongside it, in everyday settings, communities that touch the heart, lift life above the normal, and put Jesus on display."[141] There is an increasing awareness that our mission is not about what we do in or with the church but rather how we can be present in the confusion and pain of local communities.

There are moments in my journey of faith that I now refer to as 'Advent moments', when I was conscious of God's gentle leading and guiding. When I was in my last year of school and sensing a call to deeper and more consistent discipleship, there was a series of events held in my home parish that were led by a Church Army evangelist.

---

140 Eddie Gibbs and Ian Coffey, *Church Next*, (Illinois, InterVarsity Press, 2001), 20.
141 Michael Moynagh, *Being Church, Doing Life*, (Oxford, Monarch, 2014), 24.

This was a critical moment in my journey for which I am very grateful. When, many decades later, I was invited to join the board of Church Army, I was delighted and honoured to do so, as it had been part of a very formative moment in my discipleship. I am thrilled that in Connor diocese we have a partnership with Church Army, in a centre of mission in North Belfast. There is also a centre of mission in Tuam diocese in the west of Ireland and this is an inter-church project. Centres of mission are a key part of Church Army's strategy and have shaped some of my thinking on mission today. "We share our faith through words and action. We are relevant; we find out what each community needs and share Jesus with them in their context. We love and work in close partnership with the local church; centres of mission enable and empower the local church and individuals in their own evangelism and outreach."[142]

In setting out on this partnership, there were many discussions within the diocesan structures and conversations with local clergy and parishes. There were difficulties in sharing this vision as it was impossible to see what the end result would be and there were many unanswered questions. I am grateful for the trust many showed in this dream and we are discovering lessons on the way, often from mistakes or failures. In my own thinking, the seed thought of this came from the clear recognition that the difficulty of maintaining parish ministry and structures in parts of Belfast is increasing, and it is also placing a huge burden on a few, and particularly upon clergy who are offering faithful pastoral care, but at great personal cost. My own thinking is that we are seeking to find new ways of developing new faith communities, as well as offering supportive ministry to those who have faithfully carried the baton of faith in parts of the city of Belfast battered by the Troubles. This is a genuine attempt to be Jesus in the mess and pain of a community that has at times lost hope. As a diocese, we could not do this without the experience, support and commitment of Church Army. We now have two Church Army pioneer evangelists, ministering and building relationships

142 Church Army Website https://churcharmy.org.uk

and connections within local community, Karen Webb and Stephen Whitten. They bring energy, passion and their God-given gifts to this ministry. This has involved renting two shops on the Shankill Road in a community centre, with the strategic planning and management of our diocesan development officer, Trevor Douglas.

From this base, there are already different ministries being offered: helping young people to engage better with education with Transforming Lives for Good. TLG has been helping young people for 20 years and works in partnerships with local faith communities. "TLG exists to bring hope and a future for struggling children. From school exclusion, to low emotional wellbeing and holiday hunger, there are children across the UK facing some of the toughest starts in life. We're all about believing change is possible and that's why in all our work lies an unchanging resolve to transform lives for good."[143]

Baby basics is a way of serving young mums, with baskets of essential gifts at the birth of a newborn baby. These are distributed by health professionals and the referrals come from them as well. Items for the baskets are collected by different parishes in the diocese and a volunteer helps administer this ministry. On average, there are six referrals per week. This is a growing ministry and is making a real difference in the lives of those involved. Parishes have been excited and willing to help and there are no strings attached to this ministry of care and compassion.

There is a partnership with CAP, Christians Against Poverty. A life-skills class has been held in conjunction with a local parish and has helped people change their money habits. The support of the rector, the Rev'd Tracey McRoberts, has been invaluable and she has also played a key role as rural dean. There are after-school drop-ins in the base and these are building relationships with local children and families. It is fascinating observing this development in the community, among parishes and indeed in the diocese. There are still questions and confusion as to what exactly a centre of mission is doing. I believe it is modelling incarnation and serving the local community. One of

143 TLG website https://tlg.org.uk

the lessons for me is expressed as follows: "Likewise the church to-day can no longer come on its own terms, as it did in the days of Christendom, to the population at large but rather it must come with humility offering loving service, with a message that both inspires and pervades its action, to a world that is intrigued, has echoes of the Christian past in its collective mind (which too often can be unhelp-ful) but has largely turned its back on the church if not Jesus."[144]

This centre of mission is in the early stages of development. There is also the dream that sometime in the future we will be able to grow a new community of faith or, if I am allowed to dream big, there will be new communities of faith. This will be very different from traditional church and will need to be nurtured. I am excited and yet conscious that all of this takes time, and I cannot give a clear picture of what the new faith communities will look like, but the future will be dif-ferent. "New forms of church have to be allowed to develop without any assumption that they are a bridge into mainstream convention-al Church. They may need to exist alongside, but only very loosely integrated into, the main body of the Church."[145] This is a very real tension because as members of traditional church we still want to see how anything we do can help us maintain and grow what we have. That is not our task, rather we are to share Jesus and his ministry of grace and care with all. The Spirit of God can then lead us into a new future whatever that might look like.

Church Army has been expanding the number of centres of mis-sion throughout the UK and Ireland; it is investing resources and huge energy into developing these places of encounter and innovation that help people in local communities encounter Jesus. I visited three of these centres and was challenged and inspired by the people that I met and their stories. It is very obvious that one of the cornerstones that is the heartbeat of these special places is relationships. The peo-ple I encountered found in those who ministered in these contexts friends who believed in them and helped them help themselves. They

144 Patrick Whitworth, *Prepare for Exile*, (London, SPCK, 2008), 113.
145 Michael Perham, *To Tell Afresh*, (London, SPCK, 2010), 48.

are accompanied by people who genuinely believe that they are made in the image of God, and despite what schools or society may label them, they are special and unique. Many of those whom I met had already been disempowered and are angry and confused. The centres of mission seek to walk with them in friendship and celebrate who they are rather than focus on their problems. I find this so refreshing, as it is what I observe in Jesus who saw the person not the problem and sought to bring blessing, hope, and indeed, new beginnings.

"For over a decade, Nick has worked with youngsters written off by the authorities as 'unmanageable' on three deprived estates bordering the South Circular Road - the Page, Middle Park and Brook estates. He has battled tirelessly to give them the insight, self esteem and employment prospects they need to eschew criminality and embrace normality as a life choice."[146] Having read this article about Nick Russell and his work in Greenwich, I was delighted to meet him and his team. I am grateful for their kindness and hospitality in the midst of their heavy workload. It was a joy to spend time with this team and hear their stories as to why they are committed to the young people there. This is a commitment that goes above and beyond any job or duty, but is of the heart, mind and soul. They love and give of themselves to others and fight in their corner (metaphorically) and believe in them, when many do not. I was also privileged to meet some of the young people with whom the team has built friendships. They are so grateful for this safe place that is a gift to them, and for the people who believe in them, even though they find it hard to believe in themselves. I would love to tell you their stories, but that would be unfair, as they are personal and were given to me in trust because I was someone Nick described as a friend. Suffice to say, that some of the issues that were present were; knife crime, drugs, exclusion from school and deprivation. Table tennis, pool, punch bags, music, crafts, stories and laughter were all present, but the most important aspect was encounter, face-to-face, and heart-to-heart, encounter, that has enabled hope to be possible. I was profoundly challenged, disturbed and encouraged

146 David Cohen, *London Evening Standard*, Monday 27/02/2017.

by what I heard and saw, yet it was very clear to me that this is where Jesus would be and the people he would want to encounter if he was here today. This is the nub of the matter, he is here today, present in the people who serve the centre of mission, and thereby, in those who serve others because of Jesus and their discipleship.

This model of incarnation is not just about serving others and being Jesus to them; it is also about how we can be changed by those with whom we build relationships. In conversation with Nick it is obvious how he has witnessed and shared some of the most difficult family stories and the deep hurt many in this community have experienced. Yet in the midst of the pain and confusion, he also testifies to the selflessness of many, and the generosity and care people have shown to one another. He has found the very presence of God in some very tragic and difficult human stories. I would want to add, that he, by being there with his family and his team, has enabled people to experience the real presence of Jesus.

Selby in North Yorkshire was my next visit and it was a joy to meet Richard Cooke who leads the Selby Centre of Mission. He was joined recently by Amy Hayes as a trainee pioneer evangelist. Amy is from Northern Ireland and made me feel very at home by wearing her Northern Ireland football shirt! Their gifts of hospitality, soul-sharing and time were a great blessing and encouragement to me. Their service and ministry are with families of the Flaxley Road estate. They have such energy, commitment to Jesus and to the people of these estates. This is one of the most socially deprived estates in North Yorkshire. I heard so many stories of people's lives broken by pain and hurt. As we walked the streets of these estates it was very obvious how Richard was appreciated, by his constant ministry of presence with the people and the relationship of trust he has built over many years. This centre of mission, like others, is in the mess, and yet potential of lived human experience. There is a very close link with the local church and there are many activities: school assemblies, an after-school club, youth alpha and similar meetings, a converted double decker bus as a community drop-in centre and youth cafe, parent and toddler group, practical help with parenting and debt. The support of the local church has been critical and this partnership brings much blessing. They have their own website, which is worth viewing. (www.edgecommunity.org.uk)

During my visit, I was able to meet some of the young people at a barbecue. I have to confess that I did burn the sausages, but I was too busy listening to stories. These are amazing young people and their ability to do more than survive in difficult circumstances is breathtaking. I have such admiration for them, as we laughed and joked together as they supported one another. The young people were so grateful for this ministry and presence that gave them a safe place and support. They know that here there are people who believe in them, and will be there for them, in what is a difficult and challenging world. My own reflections were sharpened by the fact that, before I had visited either Greenwich or Selby, I had spent a few days in the House of Commons, listening to statistics about youth crime and employment. The two worlds screamed at each other, and I am very concerned that there is such a disconnect from the world of decision-making, and the lives of people who have to live in demanding and difficult circumstances by an accident of birth, rather than by choice. I want to invite those who make decisions about the future of young people, like the beautiful ones I met, to go and talk to those who are at the sharp end of government policy. I want others to see the amazing potential, and how all of us are made in the image of God.

The Amber Project is based in Cardiff and provides help and support to young people (aged 14-25) who have experience of self-harm. There are various ways support is offered: counselling, evening workshops, theatre workshops and informal support. They have office and meeting space in city-centre Cardiff, but are limited by the space they have available, as there are so many referrals. They receive referrals from local health agencies, and young people can make contact directly with them. This is a very important project for Church Army, and it was a privilege to be welcomed, and to be invited to hear some of the thoughts of a few, who have been helped so much, by the people who serve this project. It is the people, staff and volunteers that enable this project to have such an impact. These are disciples, who yet again, have a commitment to make a difference, by offering themselves in service to others, bringing their God-given gifts to bless others.

It was a joy to meet Caryl Stock and Stacey Bowers and some of the young people. Caryl is the coordinator of the project and her passion for what she does is infectious. Stacey is the other full-time staff member and is a support worker; her gentle, warm and approachable personality helps her as a listener and enabler. Their faith, joy and dedication were an inspiration to me. The young people I met shared the immense frustration they had experienced with the mental health services. They were amazing in terms of how they have learnt to find ways of coping with their struggle and deep pain. They have to deal with the societal difficulty in recognising and helping those suffering from mental health. I can identify with that struggle as someone who has suffered from depression. Mental health cannot be seen and physically you look the same, but inwardly the world is a very difficult, lonely and scary place. I was so impressed by their maturity, honesty, willingness to talk and passion for this project. They want more places like this to help the many, many, young people who are fighting these inner battles. (They also want a dog! That is a conversation for me to bring back to the board of Church Army!) In the middle of the conversations, Jesus was not mentioned, and yet, they know that is why the project is there. This is not about bullying or harassing people into the kingdom, but about showing them the loveliness of Jesus by love, compassion and listening.

There are so many issues that have been raised by my visits to these special places. I want to return to some general reflections in the next and final chapter. However, I want to note some issues that are pertinent to my own thinking which connect my role as bishop to these particular visits. One of the major issues constantly mentioned in these visits was the question of resources. These are projects that are run on a shoestring budget, sometimes getting funding from external sources, but they cannot be depended upon. Local churches are themselves struggling to find funding for their mission and ministry and budgets are very tight. However, somewhere in our strategic thinking as dioceses and central churches, we will have to be creative and visionary as we look to future mission and connection with local communities. Indeed, there will have to be risk-taking, spending some of the investments that are meant for a 'rainy day', because I believe that day has arrived. "Existing churches need to learn how to explore giving birth to further churches, which are related to them yet different from them, and central resources should as a normal instinct, make serious investment in those churches being born and those which are still young."[147]

In each of these centres of mission, there are similarities and yet very different cultural and contextual issues. It is one of the issues that constantly strikes me in my role in the World Council of Churches. I also recognised it so clearly when I was a new bishop at the Lambeth Conference in 2008: the need to wrestle with culture and gospel. In each of these missional contexts, there is the genuine interaction between the good news and the real needs and concerns of local community. "Contextualisation can be defined as the dynamic process whereby the constant message of the gospel interacts with specific, relative situations ... Contextualisation attempts to communicate the gospel in word and deed and to establish churches in ways that make sense to people within their cultural context."[148] We have to be more aware and committed to this wrestling with context and culture, otherwise we will become increasingly irrelevant and obsolete. There is also the critical importance of listening to those outside the church and to the questions they have, rather than answering questions people are not asking.

I found myself humbled, challenged, and inspired, by all I had the privilege to meet, the fellow-disciples who are living out their calling and making a difference. They are doing ordinary things, but on

147 George Lings, *Reproducing Churches*, 229.
148 Michael Frost and Alan Hirsch, *The Shaping of Things to Come: Innovation and Mission for the 21st Century*, (Massachusetts, Hendrickson, 2007), 83.

behalf of someone who has called them to live out his love and mercy. The message of grace that we meet in Jesus is extraordinary, but we carry and reflect it in our broken lives. However, I found myself particularly helped by the young people I met. They are made in the image of God, and yet they also recognised their brokenness. Their pain and struggle are hard to hide, but they inspired me with their vulnerability and openness. There is something here of the kingdom of God being very present. "Being broken is what makes us human … Our brokenness is the source of our common humanity, the basis for our shared search for comfort, meaning and healing. Our shared vulnerability and imperfection nurtures and sustains our capacity for compassion."[149] Jesus was present in these places I visited, and in the young people I met, and I found him in unexpected places and people, and for that I am very thankful! He was and always is present in the pain and mess of the world and in our broken humanity.

---

149 Bryan Stevenson, *A Story of Justice and Redemption*, (New York, Random House, 2014), 289.

CHAPTER 15

FROM BETHLEHEM TO...

It has been so refreshing to have had time and space to focus on Jesus. I have sought to live as a disciple because of him, and at times, in the cut and thrust of life and ministry, I have found my soul corroded and weary, with the care of the church and people. This space has allowed me time to rediscover my first love, and yet recognise the enormity of the task of church leadership. These are exciting times, but they are also challenging, and will need courage and creativity.

"In Jesus, God gave us a human face, and I can read directly in that face how God feels about people."[150] I envy the disciples, who were able to spend time with Jesus, encountering the living God in human form. This is a mystery that we have always found hard to explain. The church has had councils and synods, to discuss the minutiae of Christian doctrine, but as I read the Gospels again, the Jesus that I encounter shows me the wonder of grace and mercy, and thereby the face of God, yet in human form. "Jesus was a human being, a Jew in Galilee with a name and a family, a person who was in a way just like everyone else. Yet in another way he was something different than anyone who had ever lived on the earth before. It took the church five centuries of active debate to agree some sort of epistemological balance between 'just like everyone else' and something different'. "[151] This tension is not easy, and the tendency from my religious upbring-ing was to ignore the humanness and to focus on his divinity. In my reflections, I have been remembering and focusing on the humanness in the incarnation and that actually leads me to find God in human form. This is indeed a mystery, but one I want to celebrate, and one I

150 Yancey, *The Jesus I Never Knew*, 160.
151 Ibid., 24.

accept by faith. This faith has been worked out in years of seeking to follow this Jesus and often by my faltering love for him.

I began these reflections in Bethlehem, and I want to return there, as I draw my reflections to a close. "What saves us in Christian terms, is not that any person went to the cross; it is that this person, this man born without a home, soon a refugee, raised among humble Jewish folk, this person went to the cross. This is what Bethlehem represents."[152] It is becoming more and more obvious to me, and, I believe to others, that the message that the church must rediscover today is that we are rooted in a faith that has as its core belief that Jesus came into the mess of the world, and by his presence blessed so many and disturbed others. This was not a soft option but, rather, led him to a criminal's death. However, love conquered death, and the journey continues through the church today. That is our calling, not to stand on the outside of culture and society, and judge it or condemn it, but to be entwined in the mess, to have a voice of compassion and a prophetic voice for change. If we neglect the incarnation, we will find it difficult to be heard, and become even more irrelevant, and lose the potential to be an instrument of change.

The incarnation is critical in my journey of faith and discipleship, as it has helped me see the loveliness and strength of Jesus, the 'word made flesh'. The humanity, wisdom, humour, compassion, empathy, grace and love of Jesus are attractive, and they have drawn me and countless other disciples to follow him. It is the Jesus who leaps out of the pages of scripture, who helps us see what God is like in human form. I find such inspiration from observing his encounters with people and how he sees the image of God within them: his wisdom in dealing with situations, knowing what to say and when to be silent, the ability to ask questions, rather than always give answers, thereby giving people the dignity and opportunity to work it out for themselves. The teaching that is so radical and life-changing. His anger and frustration with religiosity and his struggle with institutions. In

---

152 Samuel Wells, *Incarnational Mission*, (Norwich, Canterbury Press, 2018), 91.

Jesus, I find such inspiration and a desire to be different. I have the impossible dream to be more like him and am grateful that in my failure to do so, I find understanding and forgiveness with the opportunity to try again. I find myself with my heart strangely warmed, and with a renewed desire to love and follow. Jesus does inspire people, and it is through us today radiating his presence, not by argument and judgement, that others can be drawn to follow. We are called to be Jesus in the pain and hurt of the world, but too often we have wanted to talk about him, or present him as a theory or concept. We have to incarnate him by how we live, and then when asked we can give account of why we follow this beautiful and challenging person called Jesus. "We need real, breathing, walking around, hands and feet, human examples; followers that are following Jesus. This is essential and without substitute. The example of Jesus, alive in the framework of flesh and blood, gives the greatest reference for potential followers to follow."[153]

We are called as disciples to be where Jesus is today. In observing the life of Jesus, he was in the places that religious people would not expect or want to be. This is the constant picture that emerges from the gospel accounts, that Jesus was in the unexpected places with people who were on the edge of society and often outcasts and unwanted. The church today cannot expect to be heard if we are not in the places where Jesus is already, in the brokenness and pain of communities and lives. We are there not to offer trite or simplistic answers, but the unconditional love and amazing grace of Jesus. This is a challenging, disturbing and yet exciting calling because we need to be discerning where God is at work and learn to join in. It has been obvious to me in my reading, visits and reflection that Jesus is already in the mess of the world and the Spirit is at work in our communities. However, too often our focus has been on our internal problems as church, rather than on how we can serve and make a difference outside of the church.

In seeking to imagine and dream of new beginnings and different ways of being, there are serious questions, for those of us given the

153 Lance Ford, *Unleader*, (Kansas City, Beacon Hill, 2012), 169-70.

task and responsibility of church oversight or leadership. Within the Christian community, there is a long-established tradition of the tension between being in the mess of the world but not condoning it. "The incarnation demands that we neither retreat into a holier-than-thou Christian ghetto nor give our ourselves over to the values of secular culture...Jesus neither slides into compromise and sinfulness, nor fulfils our expectations of the holier-than-thou guru. We are called like Christ to be godly, but we are expected to live it out fully in the midst of others. There is no more dangerous path than the one trodden by Jesus."[154] As we observe the first disciples post-resurrection, they model one of the key principles in how we seek to follow this dangerous and exciting path; we do it together. This calling is not just to each of us as individual disciples, but it is our corporate calling; we are to do this in community, and therein lies one of our greatest struggles, loving one another. There has been a great danger in the faith that I inherited, in an individualism and a lack of understanding of how important the church is as the body of Christ. We have so many different splits within the body of Christ and certainly, from my experience and pain, we have found it very hard to handle conflict and disagreement. It is something I have to learn, and relearn, that the church is so important in proclaiming and making real the incarnation today. We need each other, and we need to recognise that the church is called by God to mission. This is God's mission and the church is called to be part of this mission.

One of the dangers that I have observed is the concern for us as Christian communities to be relevant. We are often answering questions people are not asking, and, because of the disconnect, we are assuming what might be relevant. "The concern to be 'relevant' is destroying many churches, when the call of the gospel is to be 'incarnational', which among other things means we will take seriously the different ways on which those we may wish to reach are already seeking to connect with whatever they regard as 'spiritual'."[155] To do this,

154 Frost, *Exiles,* 15.
155 Ibid., 87.

we will need to understand and know those whom we are seeking to serve and minister with and to. It is so important that we build relationships with people in our neighbourhoods, local communities, where people gather, and places of work and leisure. The essence of how Jesus connected with people, was through relationship. Even in the short encounters that others had with him, they knew they had been heard and valued. I am convinced that there is a need to be able to listen to the voices around us, of loneliness, fear, confusion and a desire to be heard.

In seeking to reimagine the future of how we seek to be Jesus in local communities, I have to acknowledge that, within the established churches in recent decades, we have generally failed to 'make disciples'. There are many people who every day of their lives bring Jesus to their workplace, neighbourhoods and homes. Our focus has been on what they do for and in church rather than how disciples live their everyday lives. The focus needs to be on how we can enable disciples to incarnate the presence of Jesus in their daily lives when they are not in church or at church activities. This is a change in emphasis for us, as we need to see our church activities as the means of enabling disciples to live out their faith in everyday contexts. It also means our worship is a way of encouraging and affirming each disciple in their daily journey with Jesus. Our purpose in meeting together is to equip each other to live out our faith and to exercise our gifts and talents for the good of others.

There are ways we can help people, who are church members, to be better equipped and supported, as they seek to incarnate the presence of Jesus where they are. Too often we burden these people, who are volunteers within the structures, committees and activities of church, rather than free them to be disciples in the communities in which they already have relationship and trust. The focus is often in keeping the machinery of church functioning rather than releasing and equipping disciples. These issues will take some imaginative resourcing and planning and also we need to find alternative parish structures which are not so burdensome for the few, not least the clergy. We must take seriously this call to make disciples if we are to find ways of incarnating the presence of Jesus in each local community.

Alongside examining equipping disciples and reviewing our parish structures, there is also the need for innovation and new communities of faith. I am increasingly convinced that we need to encourage people in a local context to give it a go! We need to be permission-givers and encouragers of experimentation, as we seek to exercise leadership. There has been a danger that church leadership, and indeed any leadership, has been seen as 'a safe pair of hands'. We need to be more willing to take risks, although they will need to be done in such a way that we can handle failure or misunderstanding. Everyone's expectations are different and if things do not work out, the blame is usually on the leader, (I speak from personal experience). However, we need to encourage and foster a spirit of experimentation and creative thinking. "'Just do something.' Find a need in your community and make a plan to meet it. Identify a way to love God and neighbour here and now, and then just show up."[156]

However, there is the more difficult question of the growing difficulty of addressing the trend of decline within the churches in UK and Ireland. This is a difficult subject and is viewed differently between and within various denominations. It is made more difficult because we are a people of hope and new beginnings and indeed it is the Church of Christ. I have been part of these conversations and I can understand why they are important and yet complex. There are different experiences in different geographical and cultural settings. I also recognise that I am always someone who has wanted to be radical and have questioned the institutional dimension of church. I am also conscious of my personal history with church, whereby I have still some residual frustration with how it treated my mum. However, even in naming these concerns and issues, I still want to wrestle with the decline of church that I am seeing where I have oversight. There are increasing difficulties supporting parishes with all that is necessary to do so, from finances to full-time clergy. There are too many buildings that are becoming a millstone, and yet are part of a deeply personal journey of life and faith. The most worrying aspect is the statistics that show that there

156 Meyers, *The Underground Church*, 219.

are many more funerals than weddings or baptisms and those who give generously and willingly are certainly in the upper-age bracket.

There is the urgent need to find different ways of continuing and supporting the ministry and mission of the church in these contexts of decline. The faithfulness and dedication of these people are incredible, particularly through the terrible burden and scars of the 'Troubles'. However, alongside this, we must grow new communities of faith that will have to recognise that the needs of the people and their experiences are very different. The new communities of faith will have to engage with the needs of local communities and help form new communities of faith that enable them to find and live out their faith in local context. Herein lies the struggle and difficulty with resources and understanding of church. "Coping with the effects of decline is often higher on denominations' agenda than reversing decline. Shrinking financial and management resources are spread even more thinly around existing congregations. The escalating demands of a complex world - from safeguarding to Human Resources - make 'keeping the show on the road' hugely time-consuming. Shifting resources from ageing churches to initiatives for growth is seen as a risk. Spending on a new venture means putting resources into something that does not yet exist. But withdrawing money from an existing activity produces squeals of anguish."[157] These are genuine and difficult matters that cannot be avoided but will require courage, vision and honest reflection. I find it exciting, but then I have always enjoyed the untidiness of mission and working with people. The world of black and white answers and solutions has always left me frustrated; I prefer grey and uncertain, where we can seek to try and, if needs be, fail and yet try again. "Cultivating this practice of experimenting proves challenging because congregations have become risk averse. We do not place value on taking risks. Instead, the tendency is to ensure nothing unpredictable or unmanageable happens."[158] The incarnation

---

157 Moynagh, *Being Church, Doing Life*, 274.
158 Alan J. Roxburgh, *Joining God, Remaking Church, Changing the World*, (New York, Morehouse Publishing, 2015), 83.

was the greatest risk, and yet, as Jesus became vulnerable and entered the uncertainty of being human, the results are still being felt today. I look forward to trying to build new communities of faith, alongside the traditional models of parish that have been a great blessing to countless people, by being the presence of Jesus for them.

"Starting young churches is not just something the church does out of a missional imperative or tactical choice, much less dire necessity. If it is true to itself, and the time is right, then Church reproduction will occur because it is in the nature of the Church."[159] I am grateful for these words of challenge and encouragement, as they are a critical reminder of why we must look to grow new communities of faith. It is not because of decline, although this certainly sharpens the focus, but because it is in the very nature of church to do so and this has been true from when the first disciples obeyed the 'Great Commission' to take the good news out from Jerusalem to the ends of the earth. This is part of the calling of the church to make new disciples and in our context, I believe we will need new communities of faith alongside traditional church, that will help us discover the richness of the past, that connects with the present, and leads us to the future.

In writing these thoughts, which have their roots in Bethlehem and the 'child in the manger', I have been challenged and encouraged. It is good to reflect upon this wonderful gift of God to us in the person of Jesus. He is such a beautiful, attractive and demanding person. In the bewildering scenes that unfolded in the life of Mary and Joseph, we are given glimpses into the mind and heart of God, and yet we are still left with a mystery that leaves us wanting more. I will never fully understand this mystery, as I seek to love and follow Jesus, but I do know that he has been with me in my struggle, with my life experiences and faith. Those who seek to follow Jesus as his disciples, are called to help others in whatever circumstances they find themselves, to encounter Jesus, as the one who reveals the amazing and unending love of God. The Jesus that I find in the gospel narratives is one that disturbs me and yet excites me, he has warmed my heart and called me to follow. I believe that

159 Lings, *Reproducing Churches*, 228.

this Jesus is still the same, but we have had difficulty enabling people to encounter him. That is our calling and our task as fellow disciples and members of his church. I finish with a poem that has always made me smile, and yet within, there is a profound challenge for us all.

How to Hide Jesus

There are people after Jesus.
They have seen the signs.
Quick, let's hide Him.
Let's think; carpenter;
        fisherman's friend,
        disturber of religious comfort.
Let's award Him a degree in theology,
a purple cassock
and a position of respect.
They'll never think of looking here.
Let's think;
        His dialect may betray Him,
        His tongue of the masses.
Let's teach Him Latin
and seventeenth-century English,
they'll never think of listening in.
Let's think;
        humble
        Man of Sorrows,
nowhere to lay His head.
We'll build a house for Him,
somewhere away from the poor.
We'll fill it with brass and silence.
It's sure to put them off.

There are people after Jesus.
Quick let's hide Him.[160]

160 Steve Turner, 'How to Hide Jesus', *Poems*, (Oxford, Lion Books, 2002), 150.

BIBLIOGRAPHY

The Book of Common Prayer, (Dublin, Columba Press, 2004).

Ian Adams, *Cave Refectory Road,* (Norwich, Canterbury Press, 2010).

Richard Bauckham, *Jesus: A Very Short Introduction*, (Oxford, Oxford University Press, 2011).

Rob Bell, *What We Talk About When We Talk About God*, (New York, HarperCollins, 2014).

Dietrich Bonhoeffer, *Letters and Papers from Prison*, (New York, Mac-Millan, 1967).

David J. Bosch, *Believing in the Future*, (Herefordshire, Gracewing, 1995).

Kester Brewin, *The Complex Christ*, (London, SPCK, 2004).

Frederick Buechner, *Telling Secrets*, (San Francisco, Harper, 1991).

Frederick Buechner, *Listening to your Life*, (San Francisco, HarperOne, 1992).

Richard A. Burridge, *John: The People's Bible Commentary*, Lambeth Conference Edition, (Oxford, B.R.F., 2008).

Steve Chalke, *Intelligent Church*, (Michigan, Zondervan, 2006).

C.E.B. Cranfield, St. Mark - *The Cambridge Greek New Testament Commentary*, (Cambridge, Cambridge University Press, reprint 1983).

Trevor Dennis, *God Treads Softly Here*, (London, S.P.C.K, 2004).

Trevor Dennis, *The Three Faces of Christ*, (London, SPCK, 2009).

Gregory Dix, *The Shape of the Liturgy*, Revised Edition, (London: Bloomsbury, 2015).

John Drane, *After McDonaldization*, (London, DLT, 2008).

Lance Ford, *Unleader*, (Kansas City, Beacon Hill, 2012.)

John R. Franke, *The Character of Theology*, (Michigan, Baker Academic, 2005).

Laurence Freeman, *Jesus: The Teacher Within*, (Norwich, Canterbury Press, 2010).

Michael Frost, *Exiles*, (Michigan, Baker Books, 2006).

Michael Frost, *Seeing God in the Ordinary*, (Massachusetts, Hendrickson Publishers, 2nd printing, 2005).

Michael Frost and Alan Hirsch, *The Shaping of Things to Come: Innovation and Mission for the 21st Century*, (Massachusetts, Hendrickson, 2007).

Eddie Gibbs and Ian Coffey, *Church Next*, (Illinois, InterVarsity Press, 2001).

Paula Gooder, *Journey to the Manger*, (Norwich, Canterbury Press, 2016).

Paula Gooder, *Everyday God*, (Norwich, Canterbury Press, 2012).

Jamie Harrison and Robert Innes eds., *Clergy in a Complex Age*, (London, SPCK, 2016)

Neil Hudson, *Imagine Church*, (Illinois, InterVarsity Press, 2012).

Ed Kessler, *Jesus: Pocket GIANTS*, (Gloucestershire, The History Press, 2016).

Ann Lewin, *Watching for the Kingfisher*, (Norwich, Canterbury Press, 2004).

C.S. Lewis, *A Grief Observed*, (London, Faber and Faber, 1961).

George Lings, *Encounters on the Edge - Living Proof*, (Sheffield, The Sheffield Centre, Church Army, 1999).

George Lings, *Reproducing Churches*, (Oxford, BRF, 2017).

Brian McLaren, *We Make the Road by Walking*, (London, Hodder and Stoughton, 2014).

Brian McLaren, *The Secret Message of Jesus*, (Tennessee, Thomas Nelson, 2006).

Brian McLaren, *A Generous Orthodoxy*, (Michigan, Zondervan, 2006).

Robin Meyers, *The Underground Church*, (London, S.P.C.K., 2011).

Robin B. Meyers, *Saving Jesus from the Church*, (San Francisco, HarperOne, 2009).

Harold Miller, *Week of all Weeks*, (Belfast, Church of Ireland Press, 2015).

Michael Moynagh, *Being Church, Doing Life*, (Oxford, Monarch, 2014).

Henri J.M. Nouwen, *The Inner Voice of Love*, (London, D.L.T., 2014).

R.J. Palacio, *Wonder*, (New York, Penguin, 2017).

M. Scott Peck, *The Different Drum*, (New York, Touchstone, 1988).

Michael Perham, *Jesus and Peter*, (London, SPCK, 2012).

Michael Perham, *To Tell Afresh*, (London, SPCK, 2010).

Eugene Peterson, *Tell it Slant*, (Michigan, Eerdmans, 2008).

Eugene Peterson, *The Message: The Bible in Contemporary Launguage*, (Colorado, NavPress, 2002).

Eugene Peterson, *Christ Plays in Ten Thousand Places*, (Michigan, Eerdmans, 2005).

Eugene Peterson, *As Kingfisher's Catch Fire*, (London, Hodder and Stoughton 2017).

John Pritchard, *Living Jesus*, (London, S.P.C.K., 2017).

Michael Ramsey, *Through The Year With Michael Ramsey*, ed. Margaret Duggan (London, SPCK, Re-issued 2009).

Michael Riddell, *Threshold of the Future*, (London, S.P.C.K., 1998).

Richard Rohr, *Everything Belongs*, (New York, The Crossroad Publishing Company, 1999).

Alan J. Roxburgh, *Joining God, Remaking Church, Changing the World*, (New York, Morehouse Publishing, 2015).

John Shore, *I'm OK - You're Not*, (Colorado, NavPress, 2007).

C. Christopher Smith and John Pattison, *Slow Church*, (Illinois, InterVarsity Press, 2014).

Paul Sparks, Tim Soerens and Dwight J. Friesen, *The New Parish*, (Illinois, InterVarsity Press, 2014).

Bryan Stevenson, *A Story of Justice and Redemption*, (New York, Random House, 2014).

R.S. Thomas, 'Kneeling', *The Collected Later Poems 1988-2000* (Newcastle Upon Tyne, Bloodaxe Books, 2004).

Graham Tomlin, *Looking Through The Cross*, (London, Bloomsbury, 2013).

Steve Turner, 'How to Hide Jesus', *Poems*, (Oxford, Lion Books, 2002).

Jean Vanier, *Befriending the Stranger*, (New Jersey, Paulist Press, 2010).

Andrew Watson, *The Fourfold Leadership of Jesus*, (Oxford, B.R.F., 2008).

Fraser Watts, Rebecca Sage and Sue Savage, *Psychology for Ministry*, (Abingdon: Routledge, 2002).

Samuel Wells, *Incarnational Ministry,* (Norwich, Canterbury Press, 2017).

Samuel Wells, *Hanging by a Thread*, (Norwich, Canterbury Press, 2016).

Samuel Wells, *Incarnational Mission*, (Norwich, Canterbury Press, 2018).

Patrick Whitworth, *Prepare for Exile*, (London, SPCK, 2008).

Jane Williams, *Lectionary Reflections Year A*, (London, S.P.C.K., 2011).

Jane Williams, *Lectionary Reflections Year B*, (London, S.P.C.K., 2005).

Jane Williams, *Why Did Jesus Have To Die*, (London, SPCK, 2016).

Walter Wink, *The Powers that Be*, (New York, Doubleday, 1998).

Tom Wright, *Luke for Everyone*, (London, S.P.C.K., 2001).

Tom Wright, *Mark for Everyone*, (London, S.P.C.K., 2001).

Tom Wright, *Matthew for Everyone,* (London, S.P.C.K., 2001).

Tom Wright, *Matthew for Everyone: Part 2*, (London, S.P.C.K., 2002).

Tom Wright, *John for Everyone*, (London, S.P.C.K., 2002)

Tom Wright, *Simply Jesus*, (San Francisco, HarperOne, 2011).

Tom Wright, *Twelve Months of Sundays: Year C*, (London, S.P.C.K., 2000)

Philip Yancey, *The Jesus I Never Knew,* (Michigan, Zondervan, 1995).

Philip Yancey, *Vanishing Grace,* (London, Hodder and Stoughton, 2014).